David Mitchell

Choosing a Government

Macdonald

Choosing a Government was produced by
The Bowerdean Press Ltd
London SW11
© The Bowerdean Press Ltd, 1987

First published in Great Britain by
Macdonald and Co (Publishers) Ltd
Greater London House
Hampstead Road
London NW1 7RX

A BPCC plc Company

British Library Cataloguing in Publication Data
Mitchell, David
Choosing a government.
1. Political science —— Juvenile literature
I. Title
320   JA70

ISBN 0-356-13564-0

Typeset by TJB Photosetting Ltd
South Witham
Lincolnshire

Printed and bound by
RJ Acford
Chichester Sussex

Except where otherwise indicated, the
quotations inset into the text are taken from
How to be a Minister by Gerald Kaufman,
published by Sidgwick and Jackson in 1980.

The author and producers of
this book would like to
acknowledge the considerable
contribution made by
Susan Marchant-Haycox towards
its research and compilation.

TS

before

Contents

Systems of Government 4

The British Constitution 10

Becoming a Member of Parliament 16

Parliament and Government 24

The Party System 30

Local Government 36

The Electorate 42

Politics and the Media 48

The Election 52

Glossary of Terms 60

Further Reading 62

Index 63

Picture credits 64

Acknowledgements 64

Systems of Government

What is a Democracy?

A democracy means different things to different people. The word itself comes from the Greek *demokratia*, meaning 'government by the people'. Expressed very simply, a democratic nation is one which allows its native population – the 'citizens' – to say how they think the country should be run.

Obviously it isn't possible to sit every citizen around a table and discuss what is to be done, as would happen in a direct democracy, so the citizens elect people to represent their collective views. These representatives govern the country for a definite period of time, after which they must go before the people again to be re-elected.

In a democracy, the political assembly decides what to do and makes the laws of the country, an executive body turns the assembly's decisions into action, the judiciary interprets the laws decided by the assembly and the police enforce them. The whole mechanism of government is called the 'State'.

It is generally accepted that a democracy allows its citizens free speech, giving them the right to form organizations

Revolution does not always lead to more freedom for all. Here troops fire on demonstrators in the early stages of the Russian Revolution in 1917.

which promote particular views or situations. In countries such as Switzerland, the citizens have the opportunity to make their views directly known through frequent referenda. Surprisingly perhaps, the response is often poor and it seems that the majority of citizens do not care about the choice open to them.

Within the political assembly, some representatives may well find they have similar views on how to improve matters for the citizens, so they get together into a political party which represents their common viewpoint. The political party is a pressure group, which uses the massed votes of its representatives to advance its policies in the assembly.

Although all the representatives in a political party hold the same general views, there are areas where they do differ. Thus there are representatives of the 'centre' and a smaller number of those which are 'left', or 'right' of centre.

Peoples' Democracies

The term 'Peoples' Democracies' is used to describe the form that government takes in communist countries such as East Germany. Citizens may vote for or against a particular representative put forward by the government but their choice is narrow by comparison with the western citizen, who can choose between a number of representatives from different political parties.

Only members of the Communist Party are eligible for election because the government of that nation considers that it is acting in the interests of its citizens as it sees them and those interests are best served by communist policies. A Peoples' Democracy is therefore totally controlled by the State.

Solidarity leader Lech Walesa. In spite of his efforts, Soviet domination of Poland remains as firm as ever.

There is now an imperative need to stop the growth of government and to re-establish urgently just what the functions of government are.

Margaret Thatcher – *Let Our People Grow Tall*

Ayatollah Khomeini. His inspiration led to the overthrow of the Shah. Now he rules supreme in Iran.

Dictatorships

A dictatorship is a form of government controlled by one person. That person – the 'Dictator' has the absolute power to rule, without reference to any laws, or the wishes of the people. The people have no say whatsoever in the government, though the dictator may claim to be acting in their interests.

The dictator is generally pictured as having been swept into power by an uprising, perhaps by the armed forces.

The dictatorship need not be wholly unpopular if it is seen as a way to sweep away an old and corrupt regime, replacing it with a strong leader who will set the country to right. Once stability is re-established, then in theory, the dictator gives power back to the people by returning the country to democracy. In practice this happens only rarely.

Interestingly, during periods of national emergency, the citizens of Rome could give up their right of representation to a temporary dictator for up to six months at a time. After this, the government reverted to a democracy.

In some Latin American countries, governments are changed through military takeovers rather than by elections. Sometimes the dictatorship is stable and remains in place for many years, as was the case in Spain with Franco.

There are some economic, physical and moral laws which just cannot be repealed, even by the most authoritarian regimes.

Margaret Thatcher – *Let Our People Grow Tall*

Fidel Castro, ruler of Cuba and (inset) his supporters.

Ex-President Marcos of the Philippines. He amassed a vast fortune at the expense of the poor (inset).

The Pros and Cons

Direct representation through referendum would seem to be the most democratic system of government but it does suffer from a number of drawbacks, not the least of which is the time taken to set it up and analyse the results. This rules out the rapid response which may be necessary if a crisis develops. Also if the referendum fails to ask the right questions in the right way, the outcome will be adversely affected.

There is also a danger that the public may be influenced and misinformed by the press and media into taking a view with only short term advantages. Apathy is yet another problem because when the majority of people do not vote, the issue gets decided by the unrepresentative minority.

To avoid these pitfalls, representatives may argue that they can act in the best interests of the citizens and because they have more detailed knowledge of the issues, can make a more balanced judgment to achieve the desired results in the longer term.

The democracy which has the means to ensure and encourage proper representation of the people is a stable one. Individuals under such a regime have the maximum opportunity to express themselves and this must lead to greater self-confidence. 'Proper representation' here means the widest possible opportunity for citizens to speak and vote without having to stick to a party line or be tied to an elite interest arising out of hereditary or economic factors. When people are sieved out or disenfranchised by these factors, their valuable contribution in terms of service to the nation is lost.

The party system restricts effective free representation though it does provide a programme and the infrastructure to help to elect its representatives. From various sources open to it, the party can finance the expensive campaigns necessary to present representatives in a favourable light before the citizens.

On the other side of the coin, popular representatives can transcend the party and when they change allegiance, their voters go with them. Were it not for this, it would be almost impossible for new national parties to become established.

As with a system of referenda, democracy suffers from the apathy of the voting population. If the majority of citizens do not think it worthwhile to vote, then decisions may be made by the minority.

Peoples' Democracies enjoy a measure of continuity because they do not suffer from the violent swings of policy that result from changes in the majority political party. This means that the government can take a longer term view of both internal and external affairs, planning long term development which may not be to the immediate benefit of the citizens.

Because the mechanism for change from below does not exist, citizens come to accept the situation. In some cases, the governments actually do succeed in

> *Whenever I visit Communist countries their politicians never hesitate to boast about their achievements. They know them all by heart; they reel off the facts and figures, claiming that this is the rich harvest of the Communist system. Yet they are not as prosperous as we in the West are prosperous, and they are not free as we in the West are free.*
>
> Margaret Thatcher – *Let Our People Grow Tall*

representing the interests of the people as a whole, if not the interests of particular groups.

On the debit side, lack of personal free expression can lead to discontent. Even worse, a self-interested elite can manipulate the state to its own advantage and against the best interests of the majority of citizens. In the absence of a mechanism for the citizens to control or curb the ruling elite, the only way to achieve change is through violent revolution. Close political supervision of the citizens is therefore necessary.

The advantages and disadvantages of a dictatorship are exactly the same as those for the Peoples' Democracy. The only advantage is that human nature recognises and favours strong leadership.

Speakers Corner, Hyde Park. A symbol of free speech.

The British Constitution

What is a Constitution?

A constitution is a document which sets out the structure of a country's government, how that government is elected and what its objectives are. It also contains a statement of the citizens' rights and privileges. The constitution is generally drawn up when the form of government of a country changes. For instance, India drew up a constitution when the British withdrew in 1947 and in Russia, a new constitution was set down when the Bolsheviks removed the Tsarist regime.

Curiously we in Britain do not have a written constitution contained in a single document. Our constitution comes from many sources. One of these is the Magna Carta of 1215 which set out certain rights and privileges for a part of

Magna Carta, 1215, is the closest Gt Britain has come to a written constitution.

the community. Another is the rulings of judges in court, known as 'common law', where the decisions reached come to be binding upon subsequent related cases. Acts of Parliament are a major source of our constitution. For example the Representation of the People Act 1948 outlines the arrangements for holding elections and the Acts of 1911 and 1949 define aspects of the relationship between the House of Lords and the House of Commons.

Codes of established practice, though not laws in themselves, come to have all the effect of law. As an example, convention requires that the Queen must dissolve Parliament and invite the Party winning a general election to form a new government. If the Queen failed to summon Parliament once a year, then taxation and government spending would both become illegal.

How often do we read about people demanding their rights? 'Rights' are the privileges, benefits and protection which the citizens may enjoy as a consequence of their nationality. A written constitution attempts to set out what those rights are to be.

The constitution is not an immutable document because new circumstances and attitudes must be dealt with as they occur and this gives rise to periodic updating by means of amendments. It is however, a major undertaking to alter the constitution whereas new laws including those which curtail citizens' rights can be easily and relatively speedily introduced by a government with a large majority in Parliament. For example, the Conservative government led by Margaret Thatcher has restricted the rights of citizens to go where they will in order to picket in cases of industrial dispute.

It might therefore be in the interests of British citizens if a formal constitution was adopted, though there is of course no guarantee that an extremist government would be bound by it. For example, important provisions in the constitution of Soviet Russia were ignored during the time of Josef Stalin. After his death, one of

his successors, Nikita Kruschev, denounced these deviations both in the Central Committee's Report to the XXth Party Congress and in his famous 'secret' speech (released by the US Department of State on June 4, 1956).

The Sovereignty of Parliament

The British 'constitution' provides that only Parliament can make, amend, or repeal laws but since we are a democracy, this process does not happen in a vacuum. Consultations take place with local authorities, advisory committees and pressure groups all the time. Parliament is not however obliged to pay heed to the advice received by means of these consultations.

Nevertheless, the power of Parliament in making laws is not always absolute as can be seen in the case of the Conservatives' attempt to introduce the 1971 Industrial Relations Act.

This Act required that legally binding contracts should be agreed between workers and employers, overseen by a specially created 'National Industrial Relations Court'. All trade unions were to be registered and obliged to follow a set procedure of strike balloting. The Act was introduced at a time when trade unions were already incensed over the imposition of a wage limit.

The Trades Union Congress opposed the Act and industrial action by the miners, railway staff and power workers led to the government declaring a state of emergency. The Conservative government led by Edward Heath decided to put its policies before the people and in February 1974, a general election was called. The Conservatives lost and the Act was dropped by the incoming Labour government under Harold Wilson.

The struggle between News International and the print unions was the source of much bitterness.

There are those who believe that between 1970 and 1979 three British Governments were brought down by the trade unions.

(above) The Queen used Drake's sword to dub yachtsman Francis Chichester knight.

(below) A glum Harold Wilson drives to Buckingham Palace to relinquish the seals of office in 1970.

The Conservative government of Margaret Thatcher has proved more successful in curtailing the power of the unions by introducing legislation piecemeal. It has used the laws made in this way to reduce the range of industrial action that unions can take and so prevented a repeat of the 1974 failure.

This example also shows the way in which laws are introduced by a political party in Parliament. The party with the majority of voting representatives in the House of Commons usually forms the government and laws put forward by the government rely on this majority to make them Acts of Parliament.

Circumstances outside Britain can also theoretically affect the sovereignty of Parliament. For example, the 1972 European Communities Act requires English courts to refuse to apply those Acts of Parliament which contravene European treaties.

What role does the Monarchy play?

The Queen is head of state by hereditary right. Before the seventeenth century, the monarch's power was absolute and dominated all functions of government, but nowadays those functions are divided between the Cabinet, Prime Minister and Houses of Parliament. However, the Queen still retains links with these institutions and has weekly briefings from the Prime Minister.

The role of our constitutional monarch is now mainly ceremonial. Acts of Parliament cannot become law until they receive the Queen's assent, though this is automatic. The last time assent was withheld was in 1707. The Queen has the power to declare war, make treaties with other countries, grant pardons and appoint a Prime Minister but in practice, she only 'rubber stamps' the policies of the government.

The Queen opens Parliament with a speech drafted by the Cabinet, containing an outline of the government's policies for the coming session. Although the Queen appoints Church of England archbishops, ministers and Lords of Appeal, she is merely endorsing the Prime Minister's nominations.

There is no doubt that the monarch has a valuable role in international public relations.

Since George III's accession in 1760, the monarch has given over all hereditary revenues from the Crown Estates for the duration of the reign, receiving instead a fixed sum of money referred to as the 'Civil List'. This is used to support the monarch and certain members of the Royal Family. The amount granted hasn't always kept pace with inflation and in 1971 the Queen asked the House of Commons for an increase. In the Civil List Act of 1972, it was resolved that the Royal Trustees would periodically report on the state of the Queen's finances and the Treasury would make the appropriate adjustments.

The Queen is exempt from paying such taxes as income tax, surtax and capital gains tax, but she does pay VAT and a great deal in such local government taxes as rates.

(above) Willie Hamilton MP is not the Queen's most devoted subject.

(left) The royal family is not however short of loyal admirers – here cheering the Duke and Duchess of York.

13

Tony Benn MP was once Lord Stansgate. Thanks to the Peerage Act 1963, he was able to renounce his title and resume his career in Parliament. This is the document that did the trick.

The House of Lords

In the thirteenth century, early Parliaments were quite literally parleys between the King and his civil servants, ministers on the one hand and the politically vocal elements of the community – earls, and barons – on the other. The most prominent and influential received individual summonses to appear at Parliament for there was no automatic right of attendance.

Personal loyalty between knights, borough representatives from towns with royal charter, and the lords was breaking down and changing to a purely cash obligation. Successive kings built up a centralized professional civil service and found it necessary to rely upon the knights and representatives to extend the Crown's administration into the countryside, so some of these too received summonses to appear in Parliament.

The most powerful earls and barons gave rise to the House of Lords and the knights, plus borough representatives, formed the House of Commons. From the earliest times to the present day, there has been liaison between both Houses.

There is a Conservative majority in the Upper House because many lords, though not active in the party, tend to favour Conservative policies. The Labour Party opposes the House of Lords because the latter's membership is based upon both patronage and privilege conferred by hereditary title, rather than direct merit.

The future of the House of Lords was debated in an all-party conference in 1967 but no clear consensus emerged. In 1978, a group of Conservative peers led by Lord Home proposed that a third of the membership of the House of Lords be selected by the Prime Minister and the remainder elected by proportional voting on a regional basis. However, like the 1967 discussion, this resulted in no change.

The House of Lords no longer originates Acts of Parliament, or makes laws. Instead it deals with matters referred to it by the House of Commons, for no bill can

The House of Lords in session.

become law until it has passed successfully through the House of Lords. There is less of the hard party-line approach in the way the Upper House debates and issues are examined in greater depth than they are in the Commons. This process slows down considerably the pace of legislation, allowing more time for assessment of the wider effect of policies under review.

Interestingly, because the Lords represent themselves in Parliament, they are disqualified from voting in a general or local election.

Becoming a Member of Parliament

The grouse moor Tory (Lord Home) and the d-i-y Socialist (Mr Attlee) are no longer accurate stereotypes.

Who can stand for Parliament?

Any British national, Irish citizen or citizen of the Commonwealth living in Britain and above twenty-one years of age can stand for Parliament. Having said that, the 1975 Disqualification Act does not permit the following to stand:

Regulars of the armed services, the police, civil servants, holders of juridical office, the English Anglican clergy, Roman Catholic priests, Presbyterian clergy from Scotland, undischarged bankrupts, lunatics, prisoners serving more than one year's imprisonment and those persons convicted of treason or election frauds.

Would-be MPs must themselves be eligible to vote, require nomination by not less than ten voters in the constituency in which they intend to campaign, plus a deposit of £500 which is refundable if they attract 5% of the total votes cast in that constituency. The deposit system acts as a 'sincerity filter' to deter casual nominations. The previous fee set in 1918 was £150 but this was raised in 1985 to the present level. Nomination plus deposit must be lodged with the constituency returning officer within ten working days before polling day. The candidate does not have to be a member of any political party but in practice, independents do much less well than party-sponsored candidates.

Party-sponsored candidates are nominated by their local constituency committees and ratified by a national board such as the Conservative's Standing Advisory Committee on Candidates and Labour's National Executive Committee. Nominated candidates are short-listed by a special selection committee or local executive committee and called for interview. The recommendations of the interviewing board are ratified by the National Executive Committee in the case of Labour, or by a general constituency meeting of the Conservatives.

Candidates don't have to live in a particular constituency and can actually present themselves for more than one. Having said that, an MP can only represent one constituency. In the 1979 general election, a certain Commander Boaks fought for three seats and a Mr Keen from the 'Campaign for a More Prosperous Britain' contested no less than five seats.

Only one of the Parliamentary candidates (above) conforms to the traditional 'image' of his Party.

Ministers of the Church are a rarity in the House of Commons. Dr Ian Paisley is one of the few.

MPs and their qualifications

Members of Parliament come from all walks of life. An analysis made in 1980 showed that as many as 60% of Conservative MPs had attended public schools compared with 16% of Labour MPs and 23% from the other parties. 48% of Conservative MPs went to Oxford or Cambridge whereas only 20% of Labour MPs did.

By way of comparison, only 3% of the population as a whole went to public school and 5% to a university. Therefore in terms of education, MPs as a whole are not representative of the constituents whose interests they represent.

About one third of the Labour Party's 268 MPs are ex-manual workers, many of them sponsored by trade unions. Not one Conservative MP comes from this background. Only six Labour MPs are registered as holding business interests compared with 170 Conservatives.

The Parliamentary Labour Party contains more journalists and teachers than it used to. If this trend continues, then voting patterns may change as the image of that party alters.

76% of Conservative MPs are below the age of 55 compared with 69% of Labour MPs. Perhaps this is because many Labour MPs serve an 'apprenticeship' within the trade union movement before being put forward for election.

Chart showing the age of MPs in 1980

Age	Con	Lab	Lib	Other	Total
over 70	2	8	–	1	11
66 – 70	10	12	–	2	24
61 – 65	25	23	2	–	50
56 – 60	34	40	–	3	77
51 – 55	55	51	3	2	111
46 – 50	72	53	2	3	130
41 – 45	56	26	1	2	85
36 – 40	52	41	–	3	96
31 – 35	24	13	2	1	40
30 and under	8	1	1	–	10
Total	**338**	**268**	**11**	**17**	**634**

Table Showing MPs' Occupations in 1980

	Con	Lab	Lib	Other
barristers	54	21	–	1
solicitors	16	10	–	1
journalists	31	19	1	1
publishers	5	–	–	–
public relations	2	–	–	–
teachers	14	53	3	4
medical	3	5	–	–
farmers/landowners	25	2	2	1
company directors	82	1	2	–
accountants	12	4	1	–
brokers	17	–	–	–
managers	52	33	–	2
architects	5	1	1	–
scientists	1	5	–	–
economists	8	9	–	1
banking	12	–	–	–
diplomatic	2	1	–	–
social workers	1	3	–	–
civil servants	–	3	–	–
local government	1	2	–	–
clerical and technical	1	3	–	–
engineers	8	30	1	–
mineworkers	–	16	–	–
rail workers	–	9	–	–
other manual workers	–	7	–	2
trade union officials	1	27	–	–
party officials	12	5	–	–
hoteliers	–	–	–	2
other jobs	10	5	–	–
ministers of religion	–	–	–	2

The so-called 'Gang of Four' who founded the Social Democratic Party all previously served as ministers in Labour governments.

What does an MP do?

The member of Parliament represents both the interests of a constituency and a political party so it is sometimes necessary to reconcile one with the other. Once elected, MPs are expected to represent all of the constituency and not just party supporters. In representing them, they do not merely relay their constituents' wishes to Parliament but they act in their best interests as they perceive them, and upon their actions MPs are judged.

Representing the constituents' interests means dealing with written enquiries, attending informal meetings and raising issues in Parliament. MPs will make speeches during debates, table amendments to bills, raise matters of concern to constituents at Question Time, or organize petitions to Parliament.

Before you begin the process of learning how to be a minister you first have to become one. An obligatory first step is to become a Member of Parliament or – in the case of the Conservative Party, even preferably – a peer. How to accomplish this is the subject of a separate treatise, possibly from the pen of a Dostoievsky.

An Early Day Motion is a device used by MPs to draw attention to an issue or to test the political temperature on a particular subject. The Motion is not debated, but MPs will try and obtain as many signatures as possible for the Motion which might concern such matters as the length of sentences for rape, or a memorial to Sir Winston Churchill – and it will then be lodged in the Vote Order Book in the House of Commons

Whilst ministers have access to administrative support, MPs must provide themselves with a secretary and perhaps a research assistant from their own funds. The MP is paid only £18,500 a year, plus expenses, and this may be why some are not prepared to commit their full time to representing constituents' interests.

Some experts claim that without political parties, the business of governing the country would be made cumbersome and unwieldy. An opposing view is that political parties interpose an additional and unnecessary stratum between voters and their MPs, thereby detracting from Parliament's value.

Although MPs are expected to represent the party's interests both in speeches and voting, they nevertheless can vote against their party, abstain from voting, or at least voice doubts concerning a policy which is seen as:

– against the constituents' interests
– against the national interest
– in conflict with the MP's personal interest
– in conflict with the MP's conscience
– contrary to aims of any groups that the MP is involved with

Failure to provide support for party policies can result in the MP being expelled, as happened in the nineteen seventies to S Davies, R Taverne and E Milne. They failed to retain the support of their local Labour parties and left to stand,

Lady Astor (right) was the first woman MP to take her seat in Parliament. Rosie Barnes (above) took hers recently. Do you notice any differences?

successfully at first, as Independents, taking the majority of their voters with them.

When the conflict between party interests and personal conscience goes too deep, MPs may resign from their party, as did Shirley Williams, Roy Jenkins, David Owen and Bill Rodgers – named 'The Gang of Four' by Labour ex-colleagues – who went on to found the Social Democratic Party.

Women in Parliament

The first woman Member of Parliament to take her seat, Nancy Astor, was elected in the 1920's by an all-male vote because at that time, women had not yet been granted suffrage (the right to cast a vote). She stood in place of her husband, con-testing what was in those days a safe, family seat.

Women MPs seem to have concentrated their energies on moral reform and welfare and as late as 1979, it was calculated that of the 25 private bills introduced by women, three related to drunkenness, three to animal protection, nine to women and children and four to consumer interests.

Women MPs are more aware of womens' interests and priorities and a large womens' vote contributed greatly to Margaret Thatcher's success (see p 47).

In the general election of 1979, only 19 women MPs were elected, making it the worst figure for 28 years. The most ever elected was in 1964, when 29 gained seats.

Harriet Harman MP has successfully combined bringing up small children and a career in politics.

Bear in mind that the least rewarding role in Parliament is that of a government back-bencher, who does not even have the outlet of being able to attack the government...but is simply expected to vote obediently in support of it.

Perhaps the demands of raising children leave women insufficient time to enter and sustain a career as an MP. Interestingly, in the October 1974 general election, only two of the 27 women MPs elected had children under ten years of age.

Harriet Harman MP (Labour) appears to disprove this supposition, having had three children during her career in the House of Commons. She was elected in 1983 and became the Shadow Social Services Secretary. Presumably, if she can successfully combine raising children with a career as an MP, others can too.

It may be that women experience more difficulty getting selected as Parliamentary candidates because selection committees are mostly male-dominated and perhaps tend to see women in the traditional role as supporters rather than front runners. The Social Democratic/Liberal Alliance has the highest number of women prospective Parliamentary candidates whilst the Conservatives have the lowest.

Crossing the Floor

This is an expression used when a Member of Parliament changes allegiance from one party to another. The House of Commons has an oblong assembly and the government and opposition face each other from either side, so the transfer of allegiance from one party to another literally does involve crossing the floor.

In 1900, Sir Winston Churchill became a Member of Parliament and Conservative Whip. He disagreed with his party's policies on tariffs and 'crossed the floor' to join the Liberals. When the Liberals fell apart after the Great War, Churchill 'crossed the floor' again to rejoin the Conservatives.

During a debate on the rebuilding of the House of Commons in 1943, Churchill commented that 'the party system is much favoured by the oblong form of Chamber. It is easy for an individual to move through those insensible gradations from left to right' (referring here to a semicircular assembly within the Chamber), 'but the act of crossing the floor is one which requires serious consideration. I am well informed on this matter for I have accomplished that difficult process not only once, but twice.'

The constitutional position of an MP is unaffected by crossing the floor because in theory, voters elect an individual and not a party. The MP can continue to represent constituents' interests regardless of political party. However, the constituents, or at least those who voted for that MP as the representative of a particular party, are entitled to feel aggrieved if this happens in the mid-term of a Parliament.

The Chiltern Hundreds

In the countries of the Commonwealth, a Member of Parliament can simply resign, but in Britain this is not possible and a

When you reply to a debate, do not just look for oratorical laurels for yourself, but be sure to refer to the speeches of as many of your colleagues as possible. They like to feel that they have not spoken for nothing. If you can, pay tribute to them for the pressure they have put on you to bring about the popular decision you have just announced. In short, as my parents would have put it, remember that each of them too is a mother's child.

curious procedure dating from around 1750 must be followed. It is called 'applying for the Chiltern Hundreds'.

The offices of steward or bailiff to the three Chiltern Hundreds of Stoke, Desborough and Burnham and Steward of the Manor of Northstead were offices of profit under the Crown, though they have now ceased to exist. According to statute, any MP applying for one of these offices of profit is automatically disqualified from holding a seat in the House of Commons.

Winston Churchill (above) changed parties (from Conservative to Liberal and back) twice.

Parliament and Government

The role of the Cabinet

The Conservative Party has 338 MPs, the Labour Party 268. It would clearly be impossible to hold frequent meetings of the Parliamentary Parties to discuss a wide range of topics, so this job falls to the Cabinet.

The Cabinet is chosen by the Prime Minister. It consists of about 20 senior party members selected mainly from the House of Commons. Most of these are responsible for government departments whilst others are included to ensure a balanced viewpoint between the right, centre and left of the party. The party in opposition forms what is called a 'shadow cabinet', with equivalent areas of specialization within it.

The Prime Minister can appoint and dismiss members of the Cabinet at her discretion by a process known as 're-shuffling'. Sometimes this is used to cover a death, illness or resignation; otherwise it is used to alter the balance of views held in the Cabinet.

Since its duties are not clearly set down in a written constitution, the extent of the Cabinet's purview varies according to the particular Prime Minister in power. Principally it serves as a liaison point both between those who make policies and those who carry them out and between the government and the public through the press and media.

Although considerably smaller than the parliamentary parties, the full Cabinet of around twenty persons is still rather a large body to become pre-occupied with specifics and so an inner Cabinet is sometimes created. This will consist of the Prime Minister and a number of senior ministers such as the Home Secretary, the Foreign Secretary and the Chancellor of the Exchequer. The inner Cabinet is therefore a smaller, higher-powered body capable of focusing a collective but manageable view on specific issues.

Mrs Thatcher has appeared to favour an even more direct approach to relevant ministers but this can result in the Cabinet receiving an inadequate briefing.

Members of the Cabinet may disagree over an issue but once a decision is made, they are bound to abide by it. Any minister who felt unable to support the decision for whatever reason would be

Mrs Thatcher and the Conservative Cabinet in 1985.

expected to resign. This standing together on decisions taken is known as 'collective responsibility'.

Ministers may also resign as a result of serious errors or omissions arising in or from the government department which they head.

How powerful is the Prime Minister?

Any Prime Minister will have begun their career in politics by active involvement with the party committee of a constituency. They will have attended national party meetings and had the opportunity to promote themselves before a wider circle of party activists, some of whom will be favourably impressed by them. At some stage they will have been presented as a party candidate to the constituency, though not necessarily the one in which they live. If that constituency already has a good candidate, they could have been asked by the national committee to stand for selection in another.

Having cleared the first hurdle of selection, they will next have been able to convince their constituents that they are the right person to represent them in parliament. They must have the ability to customise the policies of their party so they are presented in an agreeable way and this may well call for reserves of ingenuity, plausibility, persuasion and personality.

For example, the task will be made more difficult if the future Prime Minister

represents the majority party in an area suffering deprivation through what may be regarded as that party's policies. It is very difficult to get people who are suffering from those policies to appreciate that perhaps they are drawn up in the best interests of the country as a whole. Many good candidates have foundered on that particular point.

Even if they succeed and take their place in Parliament, they then face

(above left) The Falklands war, 1982, began with casualties in the Cabinet. Foreign Secretary Lord Carrington and his deputy Sir Humphrey Atkins resigned.

Michael Heseltine, seen (above right) in his office at the Ministry of Defence, was outmanoeuvred in Cabinet over the Westland affair and resigned.

If the Prime Minister makes you an offer and you are not in an exceptionally powerful position, take what you are offered or be ready to return to the back benches; dozens will be ready to accept what you have rejected.

another kind of challenge – that of increasing their prestige with Parliamentary colleagues. This requires not only time, but also identification with and championing of popular causes as well as the cultivation of key personalities within the party. On average, this will take more than 20 years.

The Prime Minister is therefore a seasoned campaigner who epitomizes both the traditional and current values of the party in a way that is attractive to the public.

Losing a general election can be brutal for a Prime Minister. Here the removal men assist Harold Wilson to vacate No. 10 for Edward Heath. Four years later it was the other way round.

Cabinet minutes are studied in government departments with the reverence generally reserved for sacred texts, and can be triumphantly produced conclusively to settle any argument.

Unlike other ministers, the Prime Minister is not responsible for a particular government department but is regularly briefed on all important matters of government by a small army of advisers and ministers. The PM will chair meetings of the Cabinet and various Cabinet committees, have frequent meetings with the Foreign Secretary and Chancellor of the Exchequer, brief the Queen on current issues, receive foreign heads of government and dignatories, attend frequent meetings with industrialists and make visits both within Britain and abroad. Prime Ministers are obliged to attend numerous functions, official lunches and dinners, and make speeches and public statements through the news and media.

This last issue is particularly important because the public identifies government with the Prime Minister. Under Mrs Thatcher's administration terms such as

'Thatcherism' and 'Thatcherite' have come to supplant even party titles. Presentation to the television and press is all important and Mrs Thatcher's appreciation of this is born out by her appointment of top marketing consultants Saatchi and Saatchi as advisers.

The Prime Minister's busy schedule is arranged by a Private Office whilst a Political Office maintains contacts with the party and the constituency.

The office of Prime Minister carries with it great responsibility and tremendous power. Prime Ministers appoint the ministers who form the Cabinet and if any of them fail to perform to their satisfaction, they can dismiss them without reference either to Parliament, or even to their own party. Astute Prime Ministers can structure the Cabinet to suit their style of leadership and by subtle re-shuffling, prevent the build-up of effective and opposing power blocs.

The Cabinet can therefore be expected to give majority support to the Prime Minister's policies, the dictates of collective responsibility ensuring that they present a unified face. The Government Chief Whip will apprise backbenchers of the need to vote in a particular way and if persuasion fails, he has in his power the ultimate sanction of withdrawing the whip and by this means, ending their membership of the Parliamentary party.

By deciding what ministers will discuss at Cabinet meetings, Prime Ministers can promote issues of interest and concern to them at the expense of those they do not wish brought forward. If they

One senior minister, dismissed by Harold Wilson telephoned the Prime Minister next day and told him that, having slept on it, he would after all like to remain in office.

'Star Wars', President Reagan's space defence programme, has been the subject of much discussion between the United Kingdom and American governments. Here Michael Heseltine, then Minister of Defence, exchanges agreements with the US Defence Secretary for research cooperation between the two countries.

RT HON M HESELTINE
SECRETARY OF STATE FOR DEFENCE

MR C WEINBERGER
SECRETARY FOR DEFENSE

decide not to, they do not have to consult members of their Cabinet on particular issues, even if it would be in the ministers' interests to be consulted.

This control over access to information means that they have the power to make secret and direct contact with the head of Home Security on such matters as phone-tapping and surveillance about which not even their closest colleagues have to be informed. Under a Conservative government, prime ministerial authority alone is required to sanction covert security operations which may result in the demise of intended targets.

The Prime Minister is consulted every time a new chairman of a nationalized industry is nominated and they also decide which peers are created and baronetcies and knighthoods awarded. By means of judicious conferring of honours, they can spread their influence even further.

The Beatles were awarded the MBE at the instigation of Harold Wilson when he was Prime Minister.

Neville Chamberlain was one of the few Prime Ministers to resign from office.

The Prime Minister alone appoints top civil servants, sets up Cabinet committees and decides who will sit on them, selects chiefs of staff, the heads of our security services and ambassadors, and is involved in the selection of judges, bishops and archbishops.

Obviously Prime Ministers work more efficiently with the support of their colleagues, because no policy can succeed without the support of the Parliamentary party. This support can be gained through skilful reshuffling within the Cabinet, by the involvement of col-

The Prime Minister's influence on the choice of Archbishop of Canterbury can be decisive.

leagues in corporate decisions and/or by reference to tacit public approval for their policies.

It is nevertheless a fact that if the Prime Minister resigns over a point of principle, it can bring that particular government to an end. This, of course would be an unlikely move for any sane politician since it would both discredit the party and bring the Prime Minister's political career to an absolute end.

By now, it must be evident that the Prime Minister's authority is very great indeed and the cloak of democracy afforded by Parliament can become in effective terms, little more than a charade disguising rule by one person. However, when the government has only a small majority in Parliament, the Prime Minister may have to take external factors into account and perhaps call for policies to be modified in order to make them less objectionable to other parties with whom a temporary agreement is necessary.

Parliamentary Committees

There are four types of parliamentary committee. The 'standing committee' is made up of Members of Parliament from the main parties. Its job is to closely examine the details of bills passing through the House of Commons. 'Select committees' are also comprised of MPs from the main parties and they look into

When I was on the staff at Number Ten I remember the Prime Minister's personal secretary asking Harold Wilson one day: 'What do ministers do with their time all day?' to which he replied, closing the subject: 'They hold meetings.'

and monitor the work of government. 'All-party subject groups' consist of MPs from any party and exist to promote particular causes. 'Party committees' are made up from the MPs of that party. They monitor aspects of government and provide an opportunity for backbench MPs to exert an influence on the senior party members.

There are said to be more than 100 Cabinet committees, including some 20 or so permanent standing committees. They are concerned with such matters as security, defence, economic and industrial policy and report directly to the Cabinet.

The role of Whips
The term 'Whip' comes from the pastime of hunting, where the hounds are kept in order and prevented from running after the wrong scent. The Government Chief Whip has equivalent rank to a minister and the Whip's office contains a number of Assistant Whips. In the same way there is an Opposition Chief Whip and his assistants.

The Whips ensure that the MPs of their party are notified of business to be transacted in the House of Commons by sending out printed instructions and they indicate the relative importance of any particular measure by means of underlining. A single underline is taken as a request for MPs' attendance. Two underlines means that MPs who wish to be absent must ensure that their absence is matched by corresponding absences from the opposing party (a practice known as 'pairing'). Three underlines mean that the item of business is very important and all MPs must be present.

If the government has only a small majority, it cannot afford to lose votes through absent members. Therefore the role of the Whip assumes great importance. Similarly, the practice of pairing is only important where there is a small majority.

MPs have been known to rebel against instructions from the Whips and either abstain or vote against the party line. If persuasion fails, the rebel MPs can have the Whip withdrawn from them and this signals their expulsion from the parliamentary party. This is likely to have damaging consequences at local party level.

Whips also play a part in the two-way communication between party leaders and their backbenchers.

The Party System

Origins of the Party System

The history of political parties goes back beyond 1679/80 but it was then that clear political objectives and differences began to emerge. The Whigs were an influential and anti-papist part of Parliament opposed to the succession to the throne of the Roman Catholic, James Duke of York (James II). They were in favour of a constitutional monarchy and opposed the principle of the divine right of kings as put forward by the Catholic Church of that time. The Whigs comprised both the great landlords who had much to lose by giving up their privileges, and the moneyed middle classes who hoped for such privileges.

The Tories favoured James II's succession for they placed great reliance on the principle of patronage, whereby the monarch would buy support with gifts of position and land. They too were predominantly aristocrats but they favoured a strong monarchy capable of preserving their privileges against popular uprising.

These political distinctions were confined to Parliament until the 1830s when the Whigs (Liberals) set up the Liberal Reform Club and the Tories formed the Carlton Club, both intended to encourage public support for their policies. The

This is to Certify that

Samuel Hagne

is a member of the

National Independent Labour Party

for the year 1895.

National Administrative Council:
Pete Curran.   Leonard Hall.
Enid Stacy.   J. Tattersall.
G. S. Christie.

J. Keir Hardie, President.
J. Lister, Treasurer.
Fred Brocklehurst, Fin. Secy.
Tom Mann, Secretary.

An early membership card for the Labour Party dated 1895.

Tory Party split during the 1840s, losing some members to the Liberals. Those remaining adopted the title of 'Conservative Party'.

At the turn of the century, a new political party came into being and within 22 years it had overtaken the Liberals and forced them into third place. This was the Labour Party, an organization supported by the newly enfranchised working classes. In 1981, four leading Labour Party members broke away to form the Social Democratic Party, making it the first major new party to be formed in more than 80 years. The Social Democrats have allied with the Liberal Party to form the SDP/Liberal Alliance.

The differences between Political Parties

In a society run along traditional Conservative lines, the means of production, distribution and exchange are in private hands and compete for financial profit. The Conservative Party stands for free enterprise, rewarding people for their effort and making each responsible for their own success (or failure). Those less able to compete become the employees of those who are more effective.

As an alternative in whole or in part to a state-organized system of social support, the traditional Conservative society relies upon those with wealth adopting a charitable attitude towards those without. In the capitalist society, money not social ethics is the prime tenet.

In a socialist society, the means of production, distribution and provision of essential services are in the hands of the state. Profitability is not a primary objective but the system presupposes that all individuals have a high standard of ethics. When this is not the case, it becomes all too easy for those who choose to contribute little to take from the system a disproportionately large amount.

In the absence of a strong profit motivation, runs the argument, socialised industry tends to be over-manned, unwieldy and unprofitable by comparison with similar privately owned concerns. In principle, it may well choose to keep open a marginally profitable factory in an area of high unemployment. During the 1985 coal strike the National Union of Mineworkers argued that the long-term economic as well as social benefits of keeping open loss-making pits outweighed the short-term economic advantages of closing them.

The Liberal Party has policies which lie mid-way between the above, mixing capitalist with socialist ideas. Party policy states for example, that all citizens have the right to choose between a well run national health service and private treatment. The SDP, though founded by ex-socialists claims a pragmatic stance on most issues though it is naturally depicted, particularly by the Conservatives, as representing simply the right wing of the Labour Party. Social realism however, is probably closer to the SDP stance than realistic socialism.

(above) An historic photograph from 1899 of early Labour Party members. Ramsay MacDonald is at the left of the back row. Kier Hardie is second from the left in front, Philip Snowden is on the right.

Privatization, as of British Telecom whose shares are shown being traded (below) has been a hallmark of Mrs Thatcher's administration.

Democracies allow for a variety of political parties. Some are frivolous (above), some, such as the National Front (above right), are not.

The Scottish National Party was founded in 1934 and seeks an independent Scotland governed by its own Parliament. Plaid Cymru was founded in 1925 and favours an independent Wales with a revived national culture. The Ulster Unionists are mandated by the Protestant vote to keep Northern Ireland within the United Kingdom. The Social Democratic and Labour Party is supported both by the catholic minority and by socialists in Northern Ireland.

There are a number of smaller parties such as the Workers' Revolutionary Party, the Revolutionary Communist Party, the Communist Party and the National Front.

The operation of Political Parties

The party system means that to gain a seat in Parliament, the would-be representative must select from a small number of options, an already existing party whose overall structure, operation and direction are broadly speaking in accordance with his or her own. He or she may be against nationalization of industries but in favour of a good scheme of social medicine. They may wish to see previously nationalized companies floated on the Stock Exchange and at the same time, be passionately in favour of unilateral nuclear disarmament.

The political party is a pressure group, bringing together a number of people who can agree on broad policy to act and vote in a cohesive manner. They sell their policies to voters by means of a marketing strategy which can vary from flyposting derelict shop windows to employing Saatchi and Saatchi. The more money they spend on the right kind of marketing, the more successful they are likely to be. Would-be MPs cannot market themselves effectively without the combination of finance, established image and presence, all of which come through membership of a major political party.

Local political parties also provide a way for the public to become involved in the political machine. They have an organization which arranges for leaflets to be produced and circulated at the right times, hires halls for public meetings, arranges canvassers and polling agents and interviews in the local press. Without this formidable support, independent candidates are left to their own resources.

The best way to develop a mature political viewpoint is to sharpen it against others so the political party presents a good forum for this. In the Labour, Liberal and Social Democratic Parties, the views of the grassroots members, the 'rank and file' are regarded as significant pointers of political direction but in the Conservative Party, leadership is mainly from the top and constituency activists only make a limited contribution.

It is argued that those who lead the party have a more sophisticated and stable purview, whereas constituency activists tend towards short term, parochial solutions. Moreover a truly democratic party may well find itself at the mercy of extremist groups who are able to infiltrate key positions by doing all the work that nobody else wants to do. They turn up at every meeting without fail, and use both filibustering and gerrymandering tactics to force through their policies.

The organization of Parties

All political parties have a local constituency or area party which is responsible for nominating representatives to

Party conferences – Labour (above) and Conservative (below) are much looked forward to by the Party faithful.

national meetings, selecting local candidates for election, fund raising and organizing election activity. Local constituency parties consist of groups of individuals and additionally in the Labour Party, representatives of local socialist and trade union organizations.

A national executive group meets frequently to coordinate the workings of the various constituency associations and this is supported by a permanent headquarters office with paid employees. At least once a year, national and constituency activists meet at an Assembly or National Conference. The Parliamentary parties form their own committees and study groups and in the Conservative Party, those MPs with no specific jobs allocated to them join what is called the '1922 Committee'.

Way out there, beyond Whitehall and Westminster, is your Party – the political Party which you joined, probably many years ago, and whose name appears besides yours on the ballot paper to identify you to those few voters in your constituency who are not fully acquainted with your formidable record.

Clement Attlee, who had shared in the wartime coalition government, learns that Labour have won the 1945 election and he is Prime Minister.

How a Party Leader is selected

Prior to 1965, a successor to the leadership of the Conservative Party was decided in one of two ways, depending upon whether the party was in office, or in opposition. If the former, a successor was nominated by the monarch; if the latter, selection was through private discussion between leading members of the party.

The leader is now selected in up to three rounds of balloting amongst Conservative MPs. If in the first round, one candidate receives a majority plus 15% more votes cast in their favour than the runner-up, they are declared the winner.

Where this majority is not achieved, a second ballot is held between two and four days afterwards when a simple majority suffices to select the new leader. If this also fails to decide between the candidates, then a third and final ballot of the three most favoured candidates is held and MPs may rank the names from one to three in their preference.

The Labour Party used to elect its leader by vote of the Parliamentary Labour Party but in 1980 an electoral college was set up. This comprises the Parliamentary Labour Party, trades union representatives and constituency representatives. The leader is now voted in annually by a majority of this College. Neil Kinnock was the first leader to be elected by this method.

The leaders of the SDP and Liberal Party are each selected by their parties.

Factors influencing selection

In choosing a new leader, much depends upon the fortunes of the party. The party which is suffering from internal problems will tend to choose someone who clearly represents traditional values and is capable of renewing the faith. Such was the case with Macmillan in 1957, Alec Douglas-Home in 1963 and Margaret Thatcher in 1975. All three were right of centre and

> *Wilson indeed made it clear when he was elected leader that, since it would be invidious for him to have social relationships with some of his MPs and not others, he would have social relationships with none of them.*

> *Most politicians will be elected to Parliament as a member of one particular political party and, rather unoriginally perhaps, remain a member of that same party.*

embodied the principles of Conservatism.

When there is less need to herd together for mutual comfort, parties tend to give thought to ways of improving their external image and leaders with appeal to a wider public, such as Harold Wilson – Labour – (1963) and Edward Heath (1965), are selected.

The importance of the correct image can clearly be seen in the circumstances which militated against R A Butler gaining the leadership of the Conservative Party. His first chance for selection came when Sir Anthony Eden's leadership collapsed in 1957. Butler was seemingly the most eligible candidate but he had not subscribed to the jingoistic rhetoric associated with the disastrous Suez adventure. This earned him the enmity of Conservative colleagues and the leadership passed to Harold Macmillan.

When Macmillan retired in October 1963, it seemed once more as though Butler might be selected since he had by now gained the support of an overwhelming majority of Conservative MPs. This time however, he was thwarted by Harold Macmillan who had the Government Chief Whip Martin Redmayne, ask MPs "If there is a deadlock between Rab and Quintin (Hogg – now Lord Hailsham), would you accept Alec Home?" This provided the answer Macmillan was seeking and he asked the Queen to send for Sir Alec Douglas-Home.

In the event Douglas-Home enjoyed little success and resigned, so the party looked for a leader with a more public persona. This time Edward Heath was chosen in preference to Reginald Maudling and under his leadership, the Conservatives were returned to power in June 1970. Subsequently Heath was blamed for the Conservatives' defeat in 1974 and the party once more turned towards a strong leader who epitomized traditional Conservative values – Margaret Thatcher.

Neil Kinnock, the first leader of the Labour Party to be elected by representatives of all three branches of its constitution, back benchers, Trades Unions and the constitutencies.

Local Government

Origins of Local Government

In Peoples' Democracies, national government extends its control right down as far as the local community through regional offices controlled by central government. These are empowered to provide a local administration of national government policies. We in Britain also have local offices of central government including Inland Revenue and DHSS. This however is not the same as local government, where locally elected officers decide on policies affecting the area governed. Whereas the Member of Parliament represents constituents' interests on matters of national policy, the councillor represents them on a more local personal and accessible level.

Local authorities are not completely free agents, as will become apparent later. Their very existence and authority devolves from central government, so their policies must ultimately remain acceptable to that body. National government control is important because in theory it ensures that all parts of Britain have equal access to such facilities as health and education. Yet if that control is taken too far, it can rob local authorities of the chance to act in the best interests of their particular communities.

Local government in England goes back to Saxon times but it was only in the 19th century that an organized system developed. County councils were the largest units of local government and below them were borough councils, urban district councils and rural district councils. Each provided services at a certain level.

This system lasted until the 1970's when local government was taking on additional responsibilities and costing more to operate. A large number of smaller councils led to considerable overlapping of function and attendant wastage of money, so the Local Government Act of 1972 set up a two-tier system to begin operation in 1974. The county council would be responsible for the provision of general services such as education, whilst the district council would deal with such things as housing and environmental health. There remained also a third tier of local government based upon the parish councils but these were extremely limited in their responsibilities.

The larger cities presented special problems because of their high population densities. In recognition of this, six metropolitan county councils and thirty-six metropolitan district councils were created. The Greater London Council was set up during the early 1960's to operate an overall control over the thirty-two London Boroughs and City of London.

The structure of Local Government

In 1985, the Local Authorities Act abolished the Greater London Council and the six Labour controlled metropolitan county councils of Greater Manchester, West Midlands, Tyne & Wear, Merseyside, West Yorkshire and South Yorkshire. The functions of these bodies were distributed between their constituent councils and non-elected bodies with members appointed by central government. The reasons given for abolition were that these bodies had become too costly and were superfluous to the requirements of effective local government.

In reply, the outgoing councils argued that one body providing services over a wider area is cheaper than many little ones, and a loss of overall coordination

The 1980s have brought several local government leaders to national prominence. Linda Bellos (Lambeth) and Bernie Grant (Haringey) (above), have both clashed with the Labour leadership, while Derek Hatton and Tony Mulhearn of Liverpool (below) were expelled from the Labour Party for their membership of the Militant Tendency.

If the Whitehall machine as a whole is a Daimler, stately and effective, the Cabinet Office is a Ferrari, built for speed and action.

Riots in Brixton. Inner-city councils, mainly Labour controlled, blame the Conservatives for starving them of the funds necessary to reverse years of urban neglect and decay which they claim has led to clashes of this kind.

and liaison between the boroughs would mean less efficient utilisation of public money, plus a great deal of unnecessary duplication.

Local government policy is decided in much the same way that national policies are in Parliament. There is a political assembly or council, upon which sit elected councillors. The policy thus made is translated into action by local departments – such as those responsible for planning, parks, baths and suchlike. These are headed by a chief officer who reports directly to the councillors responsible for overseeing the operation of that department. The chief officer is assisted by deputies and there is a hierarchy of professional local government officers similar to that found in the Civil Service.

These include administrators, solicitors, accountants, architects, surveyors, builders, engineers, gardeners, security men, domestics, labourers and many more besides. As many as two and a half million people have been employed in local government, though the number is now less.

How local power is exercised

Councillors are mainly drawn from one of the political parties and represent a local community called a 'ward' or 'division'. They work part-time and receive no salary for their council work, though they can claim back scheduled expenses. They provide an invaluable link between the members of the community and the professional officers who administer services.

The councillors' work consists of attending meetings of the council and those committees upon which they sit, preparing for and travelling to and from those same meetings, attending meetings of the political party and handling problems of local constituents.

Political parties play a major role in local government just as they do in Parliament. Persons wishing to work for their community are likely to be more successful if they join a political party and make use of its local resources to assist their election. The party with the majority of councillors in the assembly can get its policies adopted whilst appointing activists to key committees where they

can influence the direction of council policy in accordance with the party's national policies rather than perhaps the local residents' interests. The division between party priorities can be clearly seen at this local level.

Parallels with national government continue in that the full council is a large and unwieldy body, incapable of covering every aspect of local government function in sufficient detail. The Bains Report of 1972 recommended the setting up of a central coordinating committee comprising chairmen of the various committees, ancillary staff and advisers. Its duties include the coordination of financial planning and establishment of priorities.

Bains also suggested setting up management committees of the chief officers of each department presided over by a chief executive officer. In recent years these recommendations have not been applied so widely and some councils are reverting back to the previous system where quite major decisions are taken by individual committees.

It is an absurd oversimplification to claim there is a clear differential between the policy-making role of the councillors and executive implementation by the officers. One shades gradually into the other and whilst councillors can find themselves telling an officer how to put a policy into action, the officer may tell them what is and what is not possible.

'Red' Ken Livingstone (above) was leader of the now defunct Greater London Council. Though widely regarded as a fire-eating radical he has achieved a personal popularity which transcends party boundaries.

I discovered that the normal, or at any rate expected party antagonism between Labour and Conservative...could be as nothing to the hostility verging on loathing that can exist – not of course on a personal basis – between the London boroughs and the Greater London Council.

Southall, London. Police attempt to control outbreaks of violence between Asians and members of the National Front.

Provision of services.

The services which a local authority provides will depend upon whether it has a metropolitan, district or county responsibility. It is obliged by law to provide certain scheduled services whilst others are optional. If a local council wants to go beyond its scheduled authority, it must arrange to introduce a private bill to Parliament. For normal operation within its own area of authority, the local council does have the power to introduce bye-laws which have their effect within the area of the council's jurisdiction.

The local council is obliged to provide its residents with access to education, a transport system and council-owned housing. It must also ensure that the streets are kept clean and well lit, the local roads and pavements are kept in good repair, parks and recreation areas are provided, and refuse is taken away and properly dealt with. Local councils will also, where possible, provide assistance to the elderly and disadvantaged members of the community.

The extent and quality of these services is largely determined by the funds available to the local council and those come from two sources. The larger source of revenue comes from the national government in the form of grants originating from monies collected through the Inland Revenue and Value Added Tax. The local authority also raises

In the October 1974 election, I toured derelict housing estates...and was much impressed by the poor conditions and the need for rehabilitation, which was forcibly impressed upon me, not only by the local MP but by a local La Pasionara of the estate tenants' association. Returning to my Department after the election I found that while I could not make money available directly for the necessary modernization, I could allocate funds to the council which they could then use to make the estate less horrible.

I did so and, though the appalling Tory council concerned pocketed the cash without using it on that estate, I still get Christmas cards from La Pasionara.

Tower blocks are one of the most unpopular legacies of 60s town planning. In spite of L.E. Jones' efforts however, this block was reluctant to lie down and die.

a proportion of its own revenues through what are called 'rates'.

Rates are a property tax collected by district and London borough councils. The Inland Revenue sets a rateable value on the property to be taxed and the local authority can set a value of perhaps eighty pence in the pound. This means that for every pound of rateable value of that property, the person living there must pay a tax of eighty pence. This ability to raise its own revenues independently of national government is a very precious one and affords the local council a measure of true independence to function in what it sees as its constituents' best interests.

Having secured its income from these two sources, the local authority then spends it in two ways. The first is through 'revenue expenditure' which covers such things as wages, material costs and energy costs. These are the day-to-day running costs of a local authority. The second is 'capital expenditure' used to fund new roads, housing and long-term facilities.

In producing its expenditure budget, the local authority must be mindful of current national government imposed limits. If these are exceeded, the government can impose a limit on the amount which can be raised through the rates. This is 'rate-capping' and it is a means by which government can control local

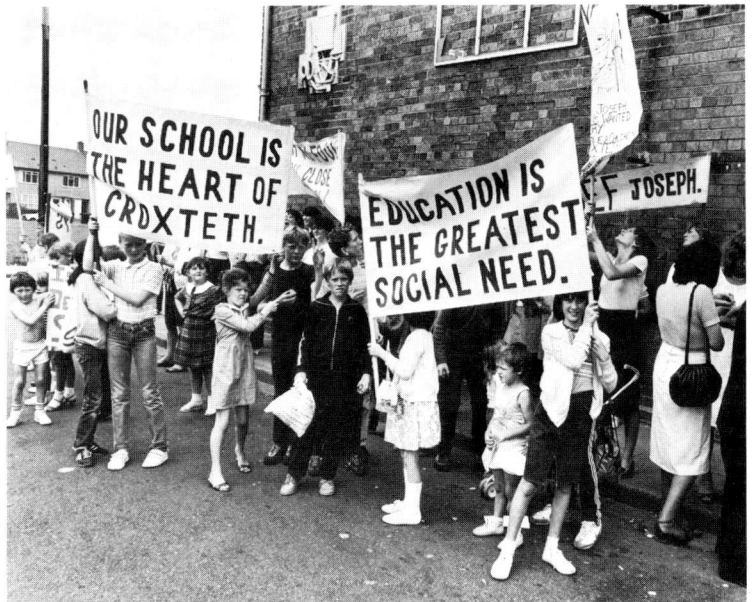

Local authorities retain considerable control over education.

authority spending.

Local authority services can also be affected by national government intervention, particularly in such areas as education where national approval for local authority policy may be needed. The services themselves may be monitored by government inspectors and members of the community in dispute with the local authority can apply to the relevant government ministers for adjudication. If the local authority attempts to act without legal authority, it can be prosecuted in the courts.

The Electorate

Who can vote?

Not all citizens in Britain have the right to vote for a representative. (Non-citizens such as foreign workers do not have the right to vote either.) Children cannot be expected to make a mature judgement on the relative merits of competing propositions and neither can someone who is completely insane.

In other countries, further restrictions on voting may also be applied. It may be necessary to belong to a particular racial, political or religious group.

In Britain, every citizen above the age of eighteen may vote, as may citizens of the Irish Republic (who must obtain permission to exercise a vote) and the Commonwealth. Members of the House of Lords cannot vote because they are directly represented in Parliament, but curiously, Irish peers can. Involuntary mental patients cannot vote whereas voluntary patients can, presumably on the grounds that if they are capable of recognizing their own insanity, then they should be able to recognize it in others. Prisoners and people convicted of corrupt practices during the last five years are also disqualified.

The 1985 Representation of the People Act permits British nationals living abroad to vote for a period of up to five years after they have left the country. Those electors who fall sick up to six working days before polling day can request either a proxy or a postal vote whilst those going abroad on business up to thirteen days before the poll can appoint a proxy to vote in their place.

It took many years for this voting equality to develop in Britain. Originally, 'suffrage' – the right to vote – was reserved exclusively for the male landowner. Some constituencies where population and importance had long since declined were still entitled to parliamentary representation. Some places which no longer had any inhabitants at all like Old Sarum returned more than one member to parliament. These were called 'Rotten Boroughs', where the wealth and influence of the local mine owner, member of the aristocracy or suchlike could guarantee the election of his sponsored candidate.

The 1832 Reform Act laid the foundations of the modern electoral system by disenfranchising 56 boroughs each with less than 2,000 inhabitants and extending suffrage to male property owners whose homes were rated at £10 or more

'Rotten Boroughs' were a scandal in the 19th century. Lord John (Russell) is saying "Reform has become absolutely necessary – the representation is corrupt – we have now Representatives of Green Mounds, of Stone Walls, even of a Pigsty, while many of our most populous manufacturing towns remain unrepresented".

Your constituents will be interested to have seen you on television on Thursday night if they meet you in the local club on Friday night.

REFORM! REFORM!! REFORM!!!

Lord John stalking over the Boroughmongers; or, the Rotten Representation in Danger.

Growth of the electorate: effect of Reform Acts 1832–1969

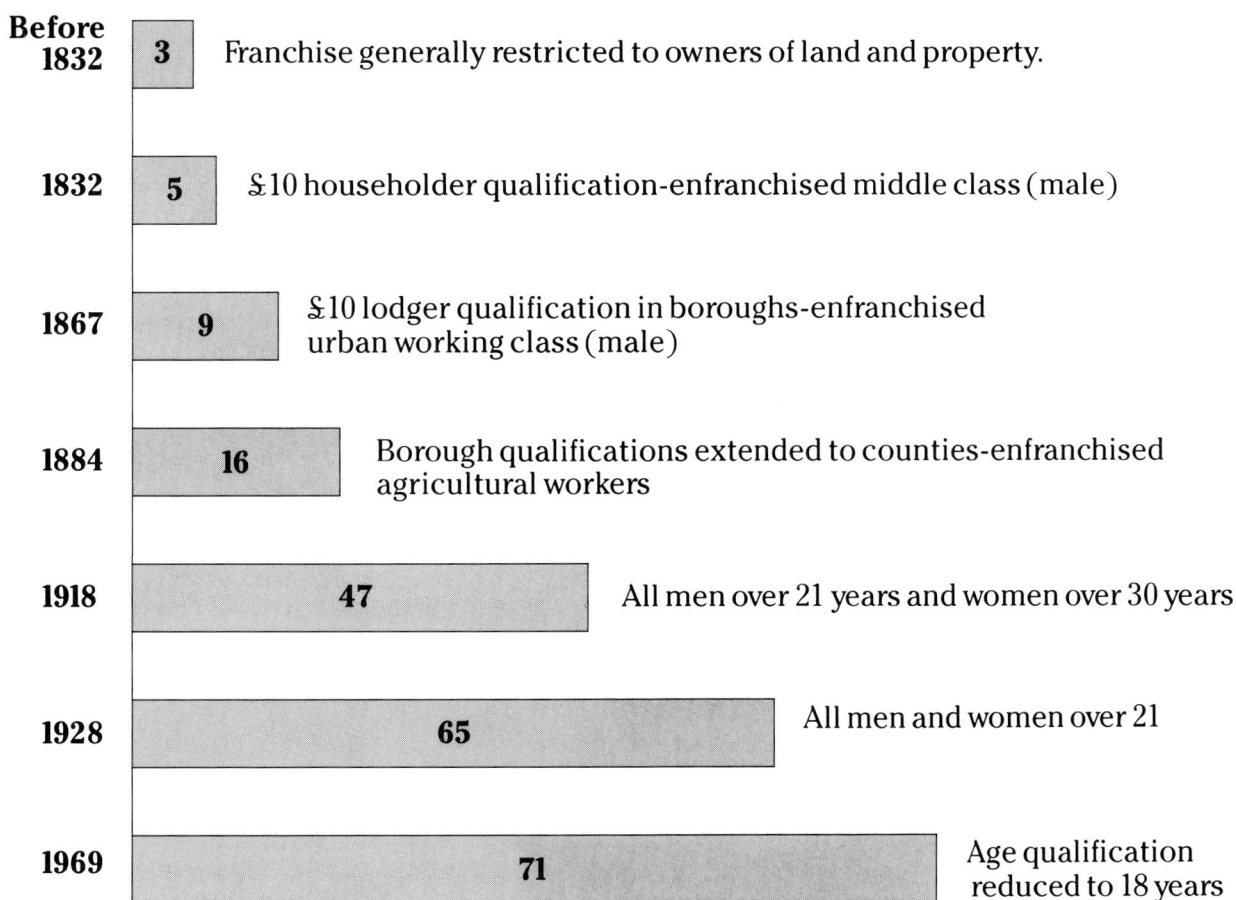

Before 1832	**3** Franchise generally restricted to owners of land and property.
1832	**5** £10 householder qualification-enfranchised middle class (male)
1867	**9** £10 lodger qualification in boroughs-enfranchised urban working class (male)
1884	**16** Borough qualifications extended to counties-enfranchised agricultural workers
1918	**47** All men over 21 years and women over 30 years
1928	**65** All men and women over 21
1969	**71** Age qualification reduced to 18 years

Electorate as percentage of total population

per year. This had the effect of increasing the number of voters from 285,000 to 500,000. Electoral boundaries were changed and 143 parliamentary seats redistributed between the counties and the new industrial cities. The 1867 Reform Act extended suffrage yet further by dropping the annual rateable value eligibility to £5. This increased the electorate to an estimated 2,000,000. In 1884, the Representation of the People Act gave all male householders the right to vote and the 1918 Act allowed suffrage to all men over the age of 21 years.

Women were debarred from voting and this led to the formation of the Suffragette movement which began with Barbara Leigh-Smith forming a committee to fight for womens' legal rights in 1855. In 1867, the philosopher John Stuart Mill MP petitioned Parliament for the granting of womens' suffrage but this was rejected.

Also in 1867, Lydia Becker founded the Manchester Womens' Suffrage Committee and similar groups joined together to form the National Union of Womens' Suffrage Societies so that by 1914, the Union had 53,000 members led by Mrs Millicent Fawcett.

The Suffragettes campaigned vigourously for voting reform and engaged in acts of civil disobedience and criminal damage. Some imprisoned suffragettes went on hunger strikes and were given temporary discharges to the care of their families. Once recovered however, they could be reimprisoned for committing further offences. The statute under which this was made possible came to be known as the 'Cat and Mouse Act' of 1913. Finally their sacrifices and perseverance were rewarded and in 1928 the Representation of the People Act extended the vote to all women above twenty-one years

Suffragettes, one of whom is seen above demonstrating at Buckingham Palace, displayed great courage in their efforts to win the vote and endured considerable brutality.

The procession of suffragettes (below) is following the coffin of Emily Davison, who died after throwing herself under the King's horse at Tattenham Corner in the 1913 Derby.

of age – a great victory for women.

More uniform voting was further advanced with the passing of the 1948 Act which removed the privilege of extra votes for business owners and university graduates. In 1969, the Representation of the People Act finally recognized the existence of political parties and allowed their names to be included with the candidates'. The voting age was dropped to 18 years and candidates to local elections were no longer required to own property in the district for which they were standing.

What are the voting areas?

The Electoral Boundary Commission was established in 1944 to examine those social and geographic factors affecting distribution of voting population within England. The reason behind this was the need to even out Parliamentary representation in such cases as Knaresborough (population 5,400) and Leeds (population 207,000), each of which were represented by two MPs. Before the establishment of this Commission, Acts of Parliament passed in 1801, 1867 and 1884 had tried to arrange a fairer representation. There are separate Commissions for

18 is the minimum age at which a citizen may vote in Gt Britain. There is no upward limit.

Wales, Northern Ireland and Scotland.

The Boundary Commission had its first report accepted by the Labour government in 1948 with the result that over 80% of constituency boundaries were altered. The Commission's report of 1954 was less enthusiastically received because it threatened to have an effect upon the 1955 general election, so the necessary legislation was delayed until 1958.

The Commission's third report should have been adopted and implemented towards the end of the Sixties but the Labour government saw that it might well adversely affect the number of seats they held. They were proved right. Tony Benn was one of the more notable MPs to lose his seat in Bristol when the changes were subsequently approved by the Conservative government in 1970.

At this time, the size of English constituencies varied between 25,023 and 96,380 electors. The average contained 64,134 electors, but 49 of the 516 constituencies had over 80,000 electors, and 58 had below 50,000. The smallest English constituency is the London borough of Hammersmith with 46,507 electors and the largest is the Isle of Wight which has 96,357.

The Boundary Commissions now make national surveys every ten to fifteen years

On one occasion, when Labour was firmly in the minority in the Commons, an ardent Socialist friend insisted to me that the government simply must win a crucial division to be held in Parliament the following night. I promised to guarantee victory, provided he could find a few Labour MPs down his street that our Chief Whip did not know about.

and at the present time, there are some 650 Parliamentary constituencies. This is a gain of fifteen since the boundaries were changed in June 1983. There are 523 constituencies in England, 72 in Scotland, 38 in Wales and 17 in Northern Ireland.

There is only one chairman for all four Boundary Commissions and he is the Speaker of the House of Commons. The Deputy Chairman in England is the Hon Mr Justice Knox who was appointed by the Lord Chancellor. There are two committee members and these are His Honour, Judge John Newey QC (appointed by the Home Secretary) and Mr Thomas Morris Hornby-Scott MA (appointed by the Secretary of State for the Environment).

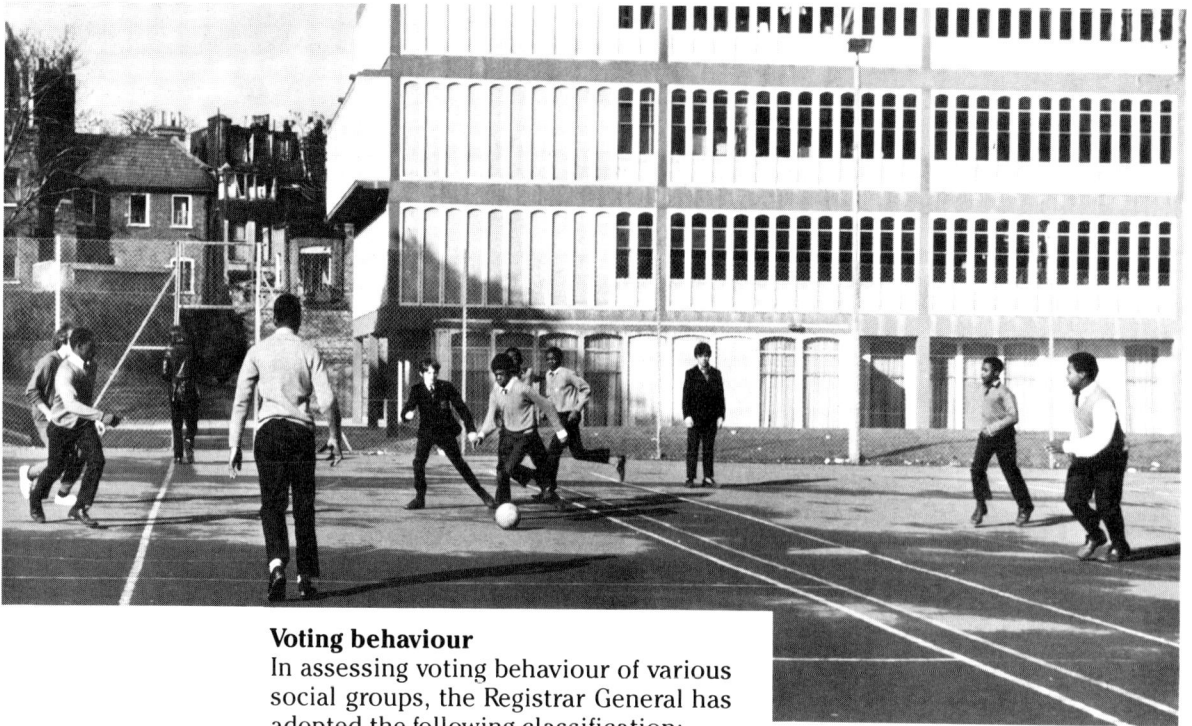

Voting behaviour

In assessing voting behaviour of various social groups, the Registrar General has adopted the following classification:

MIDDLE CLASS

Class 1 (Professional)	Includes solicitors, doctors, accountants, university lecturers etc.
Class 2 (Managerial & Technical)	Includes managers, teachers, nurses, farmers.
Class 3 (Clerical & Supervisory)	Includes clerks, police, shop assistants, sales representatives.

WORKING CLASS

Class 3 (Skilled manual)	Includes printers, electricians, bus drivers.
Class 4 (Semi-skilled)	Includes telephone operators, bar staff, postmen, agricultural workers.
Class 5 (Unskilled)	Includes cleaners, labourers and porters.

If the Labour Party was recognized as truly representative of the best interests of the working class, then Britain's governments would all be Labour because the largest segment of the voting population derives from that class. This fact had occured to those who opposed the 1867 Reform Act which gave the working class the vote. In the event things didn't work out like that and the Conservative party has been out of power on only four occasions in the last eighty-one years. This indicates the dangers inherent in making generalizations.

Why should working class electors vote Conservative? Various explanations have been suggested, one being that Conservatives are more likely to preserve Britain's traditional values. Another sugges-

What makes a person vote for one party rather than another? How many of these boys from the comprehensive (above) will vote Conservative, and how many Etonians (shown right learning to use a computer) will vote Labour?

tion is that they appear to be stronger and more decisive leaders. The latter is significant because mankind has never got away from the need for a group identity and strong leadership. In this context however it should be pointed out that one of the 20th century's strongest political leaders, Lloyd George, was in fact a Liberal. Psychologists suggest that working class Conservative voters are aspiring middle class members who vote to identify with that class.

On the other hand, middle class Labour voters are usually more politically aware and can appreciate the possibilities for meaningful participation offered by the more open socialist system. The change in Britain's industry must also have affected voting patterns in that the decline of heavy industry and the upsurge in the service sector has resulted in many working class people working at jobs once considered to be middle class. Also in 1983, twice as many manual workers were working in the private as opposed to the public sector. Perhaps these factors have affected the way people vote.

The following vote by age and sex was reported in the 1983 election:

survey carried out in the London Borough of Greenwich at the time of the 1950 general election. Key policies of the Labour and Conservative Parties were put to local voters but their party origins were kept secret. More than half the Labour voters sampled agreed with Conservative proposals and a large number of Conservative voters found themselves in favour of Labour policies. 21% of the Labour voters and 7% of the Conservatives actually agreed more with the opposing party's policies than their own!

Curiously the effect of the media on voting patterns appears to do nothing more than reinforce established beliefs. Additional information provided by articles and programmes is merely interpreted according to the view already held. The reasons for voting one way or another seems rooted, at least in part, in habit. Old prejudices die hard and appear impervious to logic.

However, the allegiance of a certain cross section of the voting population does change from election to election. This is the 'floating' vote and the first party to influence that cross section will

	Men	Women	18/22	23/34	35/44	45/64	65+
Conservative	46%	43%	41%	45%	47%	46%	48%
Labour	30%	28%	29%	32%	27%	27%	33%
Alliance	24%	28%	30%	23%	26%	27%	19%

Of all the factors affecting who will vote in what way, party loyalty seems the most significant. Even when a party switches policies, voters still remain faithful to it. This was evident when the Labour Party was successively anti-Common Market in 1961, pro-market in 1967 and anti-market once again in 1971. Conservatives were strongly against incomes policies until 1972 and thereafter strongly in favour. It would therefore appear that a party's policies are not its main selling points.

This supposition was borne out by a

sweep into power with a very large majority indeed. The only problem is that it is difficult to pitch a campaign at such a diverse cross-section of the population. The only thing floating voters seem to have in common is lack of political knowledge and perhaps a measure of cynicism.

An equally large segment of the population doesn't vote at all at elections. The most commonly expressed reason for this is 'What's the point? They're all as bad as each other'.

Politics and the Media

Importance of the media

The importance of media exposure and presentation are now widely recognized throughout the political spectrum. Techniques which are known to have proved effective for selling consumer products can also work for politicians, political parties and their messages.

However, as the parties are not permitted to buy advertising time on television, political parties have to be of sufficient

> You should plan the timing of your press releases depending on whether you want them to have a chance of being featured in the BBC television and ITN news bulletins between 5.30 and 6 pm or are ready to wait for the longer bulletins at 9 and 10pm.

interest and importance to attract television and media coverage. Inevitably the larger and better presented parties attract greater media coverage, partly because they simply contain more people to focus on, and partly because their activities have greater significance the closer they come to achieving power. An unknown political party trying to establish itself without 'big name' politicians or a widely popular cause would find difficulty obtaining media coverage. This is a real problem.

The close links between politics and the media can be seen from the number of politicians who become television presenters – Brian Walden, Robert Kilroy-Silk, Matthew Parris are recent examples. MPs who went from the TV studio into the House of Commons include Sir Geoffrey Johnson Smith, Tim Brinton and Phillip Whitehead. A media political specialist like Sir Robin Day occupies a kind of middle ground somewhere between the two with a quasi-political status that many MPs would envy!

The first thing a would-be successful party needs is a good figurehead. There are those who perform best on the stage, when the audience is sitting well back, but their necessarily orotund delivery and portentous gestures do not always translate well to the television screen. Each party is therefore advised to have its media specialists. Great intelligence is not as important as clear, concise speech and a delivery devoid of irritating mannerisms and accents. Physical appearance and dress are also extremely important so perhaps by the year 2000 politicians will rely for their TV specialists on computer simulacra of the Max Headroom genre!

Spontaneity can pose a problem so TV politicians are carefully prepared with answers to be given regardless of questions asked.

In the last ten years there has been an increase in the number of programmes covering analysis of party policy. These are cleverly put together items and present political insight in a thought-provoking manner. Curiously though, this information appears to serve only to expand the viewers' knowledge of the current political situation without altering their allegiance. Each viewer processes the information in a different way and arrives at a personal conclusion.

Attitudes to the media

National attitudes to items of political news vary. The Watergate scandal rocked the political foundations of America and brought about the downfall of President Richard Nixon. By comparison, revelations that France's Giscard d'Estaing had received gifts of diamonds from

Politicians are ever more aware of the power of the media and of television in particular. Here Mrs Thatcher (above) prepares for an interview with French television.

Presentation and strategy for the Conservatives' 1979 election victory were helped by the Saatchi brothers (below left) and Gordon Reece (below right), Mrs Thatcher's personal adviser.

the African despot Bokassa attracted little more than a 'Well what do you expect from politicians?' attitude.

Governments of Peoples' Democracies regard the media as an essential organ of the State and all official newsagencies are therefore staffed with government personnel. These ensure that information is tailored to suit the government's stance and policies. The most frightening consequences of this lack of press freedom was seen in the Stalin era in Russia, lending stark truth to Orwell's observa-

If you turn out to be a good minister, make sure everyone knows about it. Only the press, television and radio can tell them; there is no message without the media.

tion that 'He who controls the present controls the past. He who controls the past controls the future.' All traces of those who had offended against the regime were expunged from the record

49

There is frequently tension between governments and the BBC. Here members of the Special Branch remove reels of a BBC film about the Zircon spy satellite in 1987.

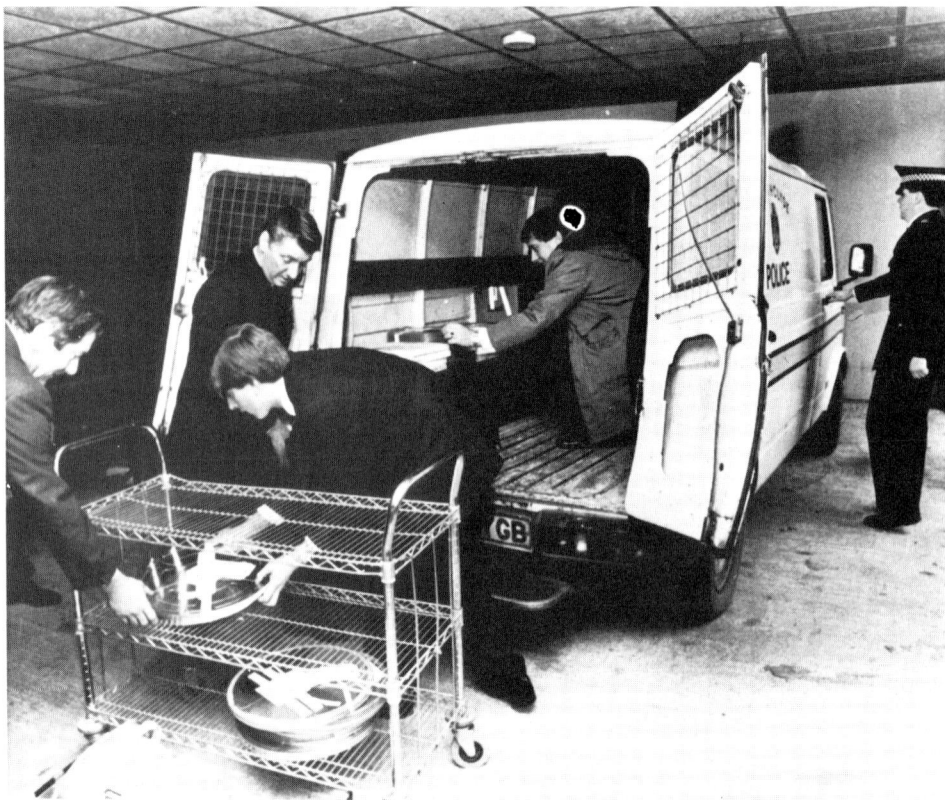

as if they had never existed.

In Britain, the Labour Party has until recently tended not to take the need for good media presentation so seriously and in consequence, it often had to struggle with a predominantly hostile right wing press. The BBC on the other hand, tries its best to be independent and to provide the viewer with an impartial account of what is happening. However, what may seem 'impartial' to a television producer may well appear differently to a Cabinet minister and the last decade has seen a number of government skirmishes with the media and press. However the Prime Minister appoints the Chairman and Board of the BBC so there is scope for a degree of 'friendly persuasion'.

It may be defensible for the government to force the press and media to tell lies by omission, as happened in the case of the Falklands War. This is propaganda, the need to conceal possibly unpalatable truth whilst maintaining the patriotic mood of the nation.

It is not however defensible for the political party in power to pressurize the media into producing reports which it regards as favourable to its image whilst suppressing those which are unfavourable. The reporting of the American bombing of Libya is an example where both the Conservative Party and the BBC accused each other of distortion and lies in their attitude to what happened.

Even without any pressure, an element of bias does seem to creep in. Tony Benn has commented how trade unions always seem to be 'demanding' wage increases and 'threatening' strike action, whereas the employers 'offer' settlements. Language can be used in this way to create or sustain attitudes of imbalance, seeming to portray one side as being in the wrong.

Television companies are required to give fair coverage to the political parties, though since the government tends to make the news, it features more often. At elections, a timesharing formula was approved in 1983 so that the Conservative, Labour and Liberal/SDP received time slots in the ratio 5:5:4 respectively.

Every morning one of your first actions on arriving at your department will be to study the photostat of press cuttings that your Private Secretary will bring you. You will be disappointed if it does not contain something about you, and upset if what is said about you is not favourable.

Remember that while you reach many many more people on television, it is the comments of the writing journalists which make or destroy a reputation.

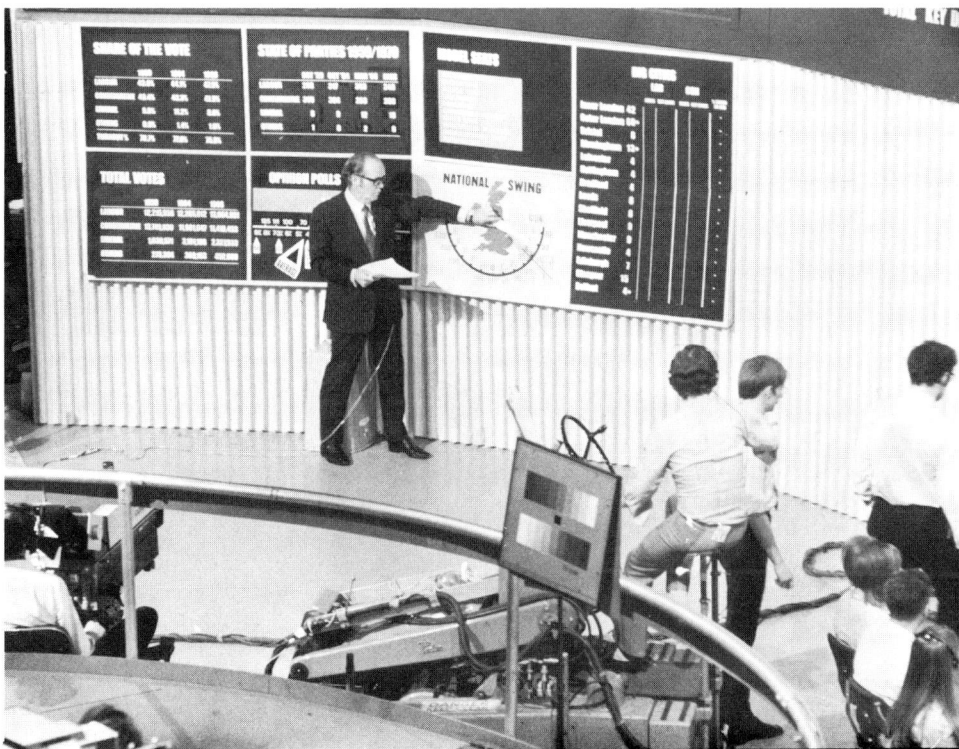

Thursday, June 9, 1983

Thursday, June 9, 1983

On election day it is 'all go'. The newspapers tell you how to vote (above), how you voted (above left), and the 'swingometer' (below), analyses the results.

In your interview do not be distracted by such irrelevancies as the questions the TV man will put to you. Decide in advance exactly what information you wish to communicate to the viewer at home, and make sure you say it whatever you are asked.

The Election

Organizing an Election

The Clerk of the Crown is appointed by what is called a 'Signed Manual Warrant' and he is responsible for notifying Returning Officers in each voting constituency that they must hold an election there on a particular date.

Local organization is the responsibility of Returning Officers who may be mayors, town clerks, or chairmen of councils. Each Returning Officer is assisted by a senior council official who functions as an acting Returning Officer. The Returning Officer receives candidates' nomination papers, signs all official election notices and announces the result of the election. The acting Returning Officer and his staff organize the paperwork, provide for the setting up and functioning of the polling stations, arrange the collection of ballot boxes from the polling stations and count the votes.

Once all nominations have been received, the acting returning officer arranges for the printing of ballot papers and poll cards, sending the latter to the electorate. The polling card tells the electors the name of the polling station in which they should cast their votes, though receipt of one by a voter is not essential to voting. The acting Returning Officer also records the names of postal voters on the electoral register sent to the polling stations, so these same electors cannot vote twice.

Each polling station is manned by a Presiding Officer and at least one Polling Clerk. They open the polling station at 7.00 am (8.00 am during a local election) and close it at 10.00 pm (9.00 pm in local

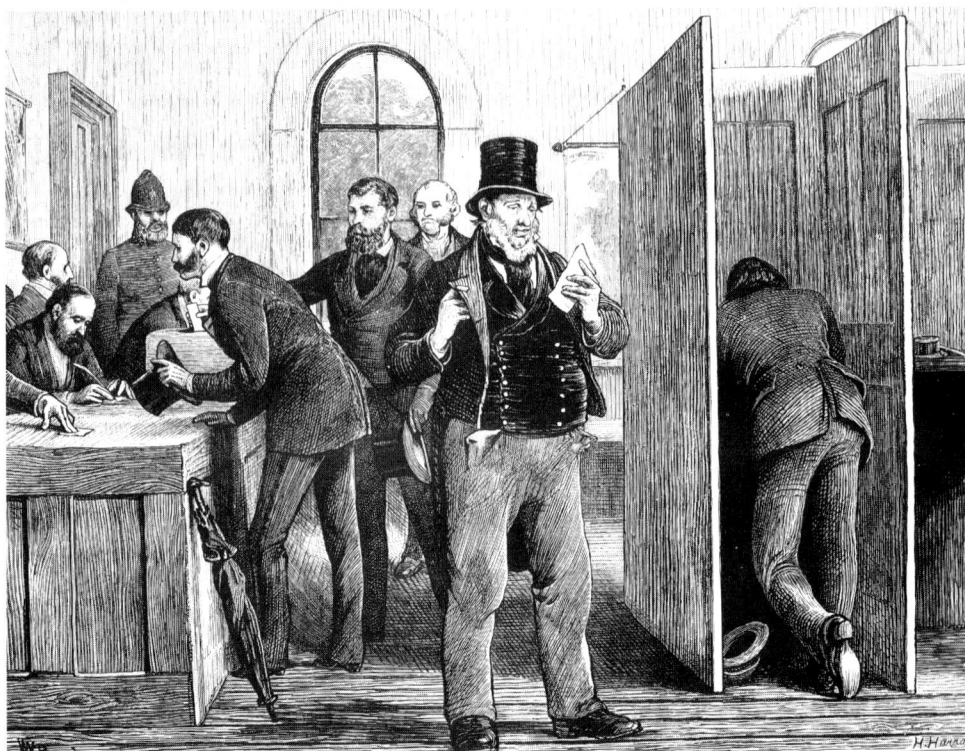

Times past: 19th-century voting by ballot.

elections) and the first duty is to display the empty ballot box to staff before sealing it.

Outside the station are the candidates' election agents. These have a register of the electorate and can ask voters for their names (though voters are not obliged to respond). By this means, they keep track of whether their supporters have voted and arrange the necessary transport for those that haven't. On bleak or rainy nights, the offer of transport to the polling station may well encourage those who otherwise wouldn't have bothered to cast their vote.

The polling station consists of an area in which sit the Presiding Officer and Clerk. Adjacent to them is a number of temporary booths where voters may go to vote in privacy. Electors present their polling cards in order to vote and if they do not have these, their identities and voting numbers are confirmed by reference to the Electoral Register.

They are issued with a ballot paper that has been validated by an official stamp and when completed, that same ballot paper is placed in the ballot box in the plain sight of the Presiding Officer. The counterfoil of the ballot paper with the elector's voting number written on it is retained by the Polling Clerk. The voters indicate their preferred choice by a cross, though ticks are also accepted. More than one mark on the ballot paper makes it unacceptable.

If the voter has made a mistake filling out his ballot paper but has not yet put it in the ballot box, a further ballot paper can be issued on request. The spoiled ballot paper is retained by the Presiding Officer.

When the polling station has closed, the ballot box is sealed with sealing wax and all documents relating to the ballot are placed in envelopes prepared for the purpose. Each Presiding Officer must in

Times present: preparing to vote in Northern Ireland.

addition complete a return declaration which is used to calculate amongst other things, the percentage of people who voted at that station.

Once the ballot papers are processed, the count made and the election results recorded, all documents and papers are despatched by the acting Returning Officer to the Clerk of the Crown where they remain for twelve months. The Clerk of the Crown also receives details of candidates' campaign expenditure and submits them to the House of Commons for approval.

One minister, barred by Harold Wilson from making a public speech seeking to vindicate his role in a controversy which was dividing the Party wailed to the Prime Minister 'But I have to justify my actions to my constituents!' To which Harold Wilson witheringly replied: 'In the last election you never got nearer to your constituents than the local golf club'.

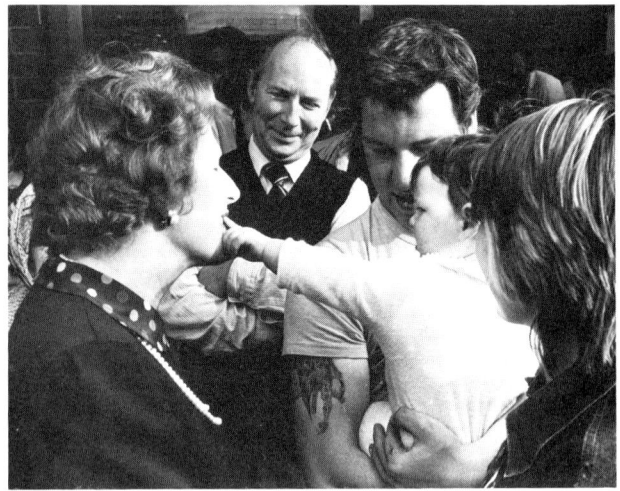

Everyone loves a baby —
especially at election time.

On the Campaign Trail

During the short 17 day election campaign which follows the Royal Proclamation summoning a new Parliament, would-be MPs set about getting themselves known to constitutents.

The amount of money that can be spent on their campaign is small and covered by regulations formulated in 1883 intended both to stamp out corruption and provide every candidate with an equal opportunity. Currently the sum of £2,700 plus between 2.8 pence and 3.7 pence per elector is allowed but this limit is regularly amended to keep pace with inflation.

Each candidate must appoint an official election agent and this can be the candidate himself though more usually it is an experienced volunteer or paid professional. The agent authorizes all expenditure and must prepare a statement of accounts which show that expenditure does not exceed the prescribed limit.

Even in the smallest constitutencies, there is no chance of Parliamentary candidates meeting all the voters, so they select high profile areas to be seen in, such as supermarkets and factory gates.

Do not look to your civil servants for ideas for your bill. Look instead to your Party's election programme. There will be plenty of inspiration there. And when you have got your legislation through you will be able to reel off the list of Manifesto commitments that you personally have fulfilled.

Their supporters will meanwhile canvass the constituency, armed with an electoral roll which sets out the names and addresses of voters. These will try to locate sympathetic voters and ensure they are aware which candidate is which.

Canvassing therefore serves to confirm where support is and to make arrangements for that support to be expressed in the polling booths. It is not to debate the relative merits of the different parties. People who cannot get to the polling stations because they are aged, infirm, or working out of the constituency at the time of the election can vote by post. The astute agent can encourage and mobilize these categories of voters to good effect and of all the political parties, the Conservatives are best at this because they have a greater number of professional agents who give this vote the attention it requires.

Supporters also drive around the constituency in loudspeaker-equipped vehicles intending presumably to remind voters that their party does have a candidate standing in the election. The same is true of the poster campaign. The object is to hammer away at the candidate's name, rather like TV advertising does for soap powders, in the hope that it will pop into the voters' minds at polling day.

The message throughout the campaign is simple – 'If you are voting Lab/Con/Lib/SDP on Polling Day, then your candidate's names is...' Any more than that is wasted because surveys carried out in Britain during the 1950's showed that the majority of voters simply followed the party line and were not persuaded to change their votes through marketing pressure.

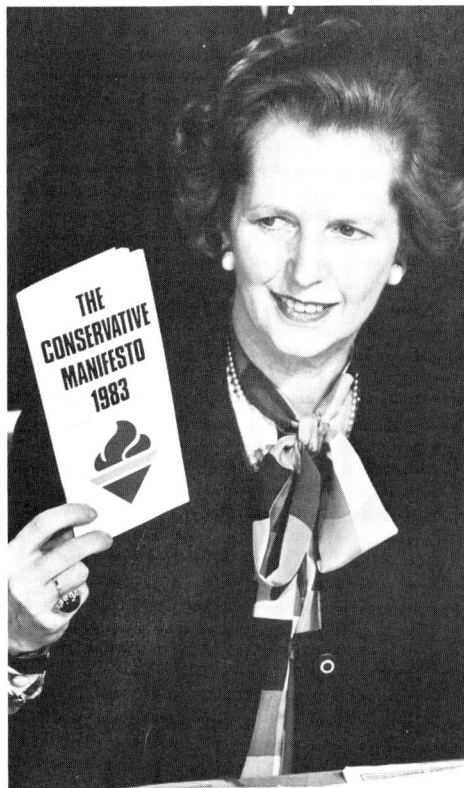

Two recurring features of general elections are Party slogans (left above and below) and a manifesto.

Slogans

Political parties select slogans which they hope will rally the faithful by encapsulating their message in a few pithy words. Consider the following for their impact:

LABOUR SLOGANS

1964 Let's Go With Labour!
1966 Now Britain's Great, Let's Make It Better To Live In!
1974 Back To Work With Labour!
1983 Think Positive. Act Positive. Vote Labour!

CONSERVATIVE SLOGANS

1966 Action, Not Words!
1970 Vote Conservative For A Better Tomorrow!
1974 Putting Britain First!
1979 Time for a Change – Labour Isn't Working!
1983 The Challenge Of Our Times!

LIBERAL SLOGANS

1964 Think For Yourself – Vote Liberal
1970 The Way Ahead.
1974 Change The Face Of Britain. Take Power, Vote Liberal!
1979 The Real Fight Is For Britain.
1983 Working Together For Britain.

Opinion Polls

Opinion Polls are very much in vogue as a barometer of voting intent. In terms of accuracy, they do sometimes attain the standard of weather reports. The statistical side of their operation is admirably managed with a view to obtaining a representative sample but it is perhaps in the psychological approach that they suffer most. Restricted choice questions produce limited data that can be easily misinterpreted. In defence of such polls however, it must be said that they are reporting on very small voting shifts which do have major effects upon representation.

Elections are held not more than five years apart, though sometimes they may be closer together than that. The government in power selects the date of election to give themselves the maximum possible advantage. After all, it is better to go for a general election whilst the voters are still clapping. Despite this uncertainty, the political parties decide the issues to figure in their campaigns well in advance so that by the time the campaign begins, the policies are already known to the electorate. A 'manifesto' is a summary of the policies the party will pursue in the coming years if it wins the election.

AN ELECTION CONTEST FIFTY YEARS AGO: THE POPULAR CANDIDATE.
DRAWN BY KENNY MEADOWS.
From the Illustrated London News, Aug. 7, 1847.

AN ELECTION CONTEST FIFTY YEARS AGO: THE UNPOPULAR CANDIDATE.
DRAWN BY KENNY MEADOWS.
From the Illustrated London News, Aug. 7, 1847.

The Outcome

The British system of electing MPs uses a principle referred to as 'first past the post'. What this means is that the candidate who gains more votes than his or her rivals in that constituency is declared the winner. There are no prizes for coming second or third. We are the only country in Europe to use what would at first glance appear to be a fair and proper system of electing representatives. Closer examination however reveals a number of factors worth pondering.

If the choice for the electorate is between two candidates, perhaps Labour and Conservative, then the one receiving the greater number of votes cast clearly has the majority. If only a handful of votes separates winner from loser, then a large number of voters will not have the representation of their choice.

Where there are three parties, then if 30% of the electors voted for Party 'A's candidate, 30% for Party 'B's and 40% for Party 'C's, then Party 'C's candidate would win by getting more votes than either of the other two, yet they would not have a majority of votes cast. Only 40% of voters in that hypothetical constituency will have the candidate of their choice. As a matter of fact, for more than fifty years, Britain's successive governments have not succeeded in receiving even 50% of the total number of votes cast.

The first past the post system is particularly hard on the Liberal/SDP Alliance which succeeded in gaining 25.4% of the votes cast in the 1983 general election as against 27.6% of Labour votes and 42.4% of Conservative votes. Despite the fact that only 2.2% separated Alliance and Labour votes, Labour got 209 seats and the Alliance received a paltry 23. However, if the Alliance succeeds in gaining above 33% of the votes at the next general election, their representation will increase dramatically.

The following table refers to the UK general election results of 9th June 1983:

PARTY	Total Votes	% Share of total	Number of Seats (MPs)
Conservative	13,012,602	42.4	397
Labour	8,457,124	27.6	209
Liberal/SDP Alliance	7,780,587	25.4	23
Scottish Nationalist	331,975	1.1	2
Plaid Cymru	125,309	0.4	2
Others	963,308	3.1	17

This Labour poster seems to have something for everybody.

These figures show the dramatic effects that even small percentage differences can have on the number of seats won in the first past the post system and it is for this reason that political parties encourage unity at all costs. If they split they are sure to give victory to the opposing party so despite internal differences all political parties strive to present an image of coherence and unanimity.

Perhaps if the system were replaced, we might see parties splitting up into smaller groups and if this happened, instead of agreements being reached internally within each party, open discussion and debate would have to take place between groups on the floor of the House of Commons.

The first past the post system therefore usually does lead to a majority party in Parliament capable of governing the country decisively, without the need constantly to dilute or adjust its policies to suit those alliances essential for a voting majority.

Those who complain loudest about the system are those who suffer worst from it. The government elected by it is hardly likely to want it changed and until they do, the first past the post system will remain; but what are the alternatives?

France has used the 'second ballot system' for over 40 years. This system takes into account competition between two or more parties and if the first round of polling does not confer a greater than 50% majority on any one candidate, then a second ballot is held shortly after-

wards. Before this proceeds, those parties with the lowest scores drop out and urge their voters to support one of the leading groups.

The 'party list' method is used in Israel and requires each party to submit a list of its candidates. Electors are asked to vote for a party rather than individual MPs. Incoming votes are counted and according to the percentage of votes polled by each party, a corresponding number of names is taken from the parties' list. Therefore a party with 45% of the votes would have 45% of representation in the government.

The disadvantages of this system are that it forces voters to accept candidates in the order that the party lists them, causing conflicts between personal and party loyalties. West Germany has recognized these objections and uses an ingenious dual system of voting which incorporates both first past the post and a proportional system.

The 'alternate voting system' is used to elect members to the lower house of the Australian Parliament. Voters do not mark their favoured candidate with a cross but rather indicate their choice in a list of preferences. If no candidate gets more than 50% of the first choices, then the least supported candidate is eliminated and their second preferences awarded to the surviving candidates. A second count is then taken and if this too produces no majority candidate, the next lowest would be dropped and their second preferences awarded and so it continues

until a majority is reached. This system was nearly introduced in 1931 by the Labour Government but it stalled in the economic crisis of that year.

The 'single transferable vote system' is used in the Republic of Ireland and like the alternate voting method described above, voters rank their preferences. In this case however, the political party can nominate more than one candidate for each constituency so there is not only competition between the party but between the candidates from the same party. Votes are counted according to a quota system expressed by the equation:

$$\frac{P + 1}{n + 1}$$

where 'P' is the number of votes cast and 'n' is the number of members contesting that seat.

Those candidates exceeding the quota are declared elected and any surplus votes they have are redistributed according to the listed second preferences. Those at the bottom are eliminated and their second preferences reallocated and by this dual process, counting continues until the correct number of candidates is elected.

Despite the complexities and drawbacks of these alternatives, the Liberal/ SDP Alliance has pledged to introduce proportional representation if they win a general election.

A Coalition Government?
If the Liberal/Social Democrat Alliance takes a large share of votes at a general election, then once that share reaches a third of those cast, it will enter Parliament with a sufficient number of new seats to give it a major role in the governing of Britain. It may well be that by throwing its weight behind either the Conservative or Labour Party, it will give them the majority.

This siding with another party happened in 1977 when the Labour government was obliged to enter into a pact with the Liberals – the 'Lib/Lab Pact'. This continued until Labour failed to deliver proportional representation. A more intimate form of siding occurs when in order to persuade the other party to cooperate, its members are offered ministerial posts within a coalition government.

Britain has had coalition governments before and with the exception of the 1940 – 45 wartime coalition, they have not proved successful.

Inter-party disagreement is a major problem to be faced in a coalition government and it might well be that the process of governing would involve the coalition in endless wrangling. Long-term planning would be one of the areas badly affected.

It is always a good idea to remember that by-elections and local elections are in the offing. Their arrival may even stimulate you into making decisions that have been hanging fire.

Reporting the Outcome

Counting begins the minute ballot boxes are received at the counting centres. They are unsealed under the watchful eyes of supervisors whose first job is to confirm that the number of votes recorded by the Presiding Officer matches the number of ballot papers in the box. The papers are then sorted by counting assistants into separate piles for each candidate, with counting agents checking to make sure the papers don't go into the wrong pile.

Up to 50 counting agents are required to process the return from an average constituency and less than two hours after the polling stations close, the first results are being announced by the returning officer for that constituency.

If less than a thousand votes separate the candidates, or if a small number of votes can make the difference between a candidate keeping or losing his deposit, a recount takes place. Peterborough had no less than seven recounts in the 1966 election and eight and a half hours later with both parties having been declared winner several times over, the Conservatives won with a majority of just two votes!

When there is a clear majority in favour of the incumbent government, the Prime Minister remains at 10 Downing Street. If a new party is elected, the outgoing Prime Minister quits Downing Street and requests a Royal Audience during which their resignation is tendered. The incoming Prime Minister is then summoned by the Queen and presented with the seals of office.

Glossary of Terms

Act: An Act of Parliament is a law passed by both Houses of Parliament and given the Royal Assent (see *Bill* and *Statute* below).

Activist: An active member of a political party, usually, though not always, associated with the more extreme aspects, right or left, of the party's political beliefs.

Allegiance: Loyalty to a cause or party.

Amendment: An alteration to one or more clauses of a Bill (see *Bill* below).

Backbencher: A member of Parliament who has no official post either in government or in opposition.

Ballot: The ballot was originally a means of voting using small balls deposited in a box. It now refers to the process of voting in any election.

Bill: A Bill is technically the draft of an Act of Parliament submitted to the House of Commons for discussion and adoption as an Act (see *Act* above)

Bolsheviks: Lenin's followers in the Russian Revolution of 1917. They subsequently became the official Russian Communist Party.

Bribery Oath: A voter's sworn declaration that his vote is freely given and not the result of bribery. The oath is not required unless all other voters have also been instructed to take it.

Canvassing: Calling on householders to obtain support for a candidate in an election.

Capitalism: A way of organizing society based on the individual's unrestricted right to acquire wealth.

Chancellor of the Exchequer: The government minister responsible for controlling the nation's finances.

Coalition: When opposing political parties combine to form a government. This usually occurs when neither has an overall majority.

Constituency: The area represented in Parliament by a Member of Parliament.

Constitutional Monarch: A King or Queen who, as in the United Kingdom, has no actual power and whose role in the process of government is mainly symbolic and ceremonial.

Count: The point when voting has been completed after an election and the votes are counted.

Deposit: A fee of £500 is paid by a prospective parliamentary candidate to the returning officer at the beginning of an election campaign. The candidate has to obtain 5% of the votes to have the deposit returned. In the past a candidate paid £150 and had to gain 12.5% of the vote. This was changed by the 1985 Representation of the People Act.

Electoral Register: The list of those entitled to vote in a general election.

Filibuster: This is a device whereby, in the course of a parliamentary debate, MPs opposing a measure keep talking in the hope that the measure will fail for lack of time.

Foreign Secretary: The government minister responsible for Britain's relationships with other countries.

Franchise: The right to vote. Age and residence requirements qualify a person to vote in a constituency. At one time the value of property, sex and a university degree entitled a person to vote.

Gerrymandering: This term is used to denote unfair or corrupt electoral practice leading to the election of a candidate who would not otherwise have won.

Home Secretary: The government minister responsible, amongst other things, for law and order and broadcasting.

Hung Parliament: When no party has a majority in the House of Commons.

Inland Revenue: The branch of the civil service responsible for the collection of taxes.

Jingoism: Warmongering disguised as patriotism.

Kissing hands: After a general election, both the incoming and the outgoing Prime Minister have an audience with the Monarch at which they either give up or receive the seals of office. At the end of the audience they are supposed to kiss the Monarch's hands.

Lord of Appeal: A Law Lord who sits either in the Court of Appeal or on the judicial committee of the House of Lords.

Manifesto: The document issued by each party at the start of an election campaign containing the policies and measures it plans to enact if it wins.

Marginal seat: A constituency held by a small majority which could go either way in a general election.

Minister: A member of the government entrusted with responsibility for the whole or part of one of the Departments of State. Senior ministers are also members of the Cabinet.

Media: The press, television, radio and films.

Nationalized Industry: A business or company owned by the State and financed by the government which therefore takes any profits and is responsible for any losses.

1922 Committee: An association of back-bench Conservative MPs.

Nomination: To enter someone as a candidate for an election.

Opinion Poll: A way of predicting the outcome of an election by asking a representative sample how they plan to vote.

Postal vote: Permitted in certain circumstances to people unable to vote in their own constituency. Applies particularly to seamen.

Proxy vote: In certain circumstances if a person is unable to vote themselves, they can nominate someone (their proxy) to vote for them.

Referendum: When the whole electorate is asked to vote on an issue not directly related to a change in government.

Returning Officer: Usually the mayor or a senior council member in a constituency, responsible for the machinery and smooth running of the election.

Royal Audience: An interview with the Monarch.

Shadow: The shadow Cabinet consists of leading members of the opposition each with responsibilities which mirror or 'shadow' those of government ministers.

Socialism: A way of organizing society based on State ownership of land, capital and the means of production and fair distribution of all benefits amongst the members of the society.

Speaker: An MP who is not active in party politics, but presides over sittings of the House of Commons.

Statute: Another word for an Act of Parliament.

Suffrage: The right to vote.

Swing: Formula for measuring percentage increase in votes accruing to any party during an election.

Further reading

Jean Blondel, *Voters, Parties and Leaders* (Penguin, 1975)

F.N. Norman, *Mastering British Politics* (Macmillan, 1985)

Bill Jones and Dennis Kavanagh (eds) *British Politics Today* (Manchester University Press, 1987)

P.J. Madgwick, D. Steeds and L.J. Williams, *Britain Since 1945* (Hutchinson, 1982)

P.J. Madgwick, *Introduction to British Politics* (2nd edition) (Hutchinson, 1982)

Michael Moran, *Politics & Society in Britain: An Introduction* (Macmillan, 1985)

Anne Sloman & Hugo Young, *The Thatcher Phenomenon* (BBC 1986)

Alan Sked and Chris Cook, *Post-War Britain* (Penguin, 1984)

These are all available in paperback.

Index

The numbers in **bold** refer to illustrations and captions

Acts of Parliament 10, 12, 14
    see also names of Acts
all-party subject groups 29
'alternative voting' system 57
ambassadors 28
Astor, Nancy 21
Atkins, Sir Humphrey **25**
Attlee, Clement **16**, **34**
Australia 57

Bains Report 39
ballot papers 53
Barnes, Rosie **21**
BBC 50
Beatles **27**
Becker, Lydia 43
Bellos, Linda **37**
Benn, Tony **14**, 45, 50
bishops 28
Boaks, William G 17
Bokassa, Jean-Bédel 49
Boundary Commission 44–5
Brighton bombing **29**
Brinton, Tim
British Telecom **31**
Brixton riots **38**
Butler, Richard A 35

Cabinet: committees 28, 29;
    composition 24; inner 24
Canterbury, Archbishop of **28**
canvassing 54
capitalism 31
Carrington, Lord **25**
Castro, Fidel **7**
'Cat and Mouse Act' 1913 43
Chamberlain, Neville **28**
Chichester, Sir Francis **12**
Chiltern Hundreds 23
Churchill, Sir Winston 20, 23
Civil List 13
Civil Service 28, 38
Clerk of the Crown 52, 53
coalition government 58
codes of practice 10
collective responsibility 25
committees: Cabinet 28;
    parliamentary 28–9, 33
common law 10
Commons, House of 10, 14, 23, 28, 53
    see also Parliament
Communist Party 5, 32

conferences, Party 32
Conservative: government 10, 11, 12,
    26, 27; Party 14, 18–19, 22, 31–5,
    46–7, 54, 55
constituency 17, 25, 32, 45, 54
constitution 10–15
councillors, local 36, 38
county council 36
'Crossing the floor' 23
Cuba **7**

Davison, Emily **44**
Davies, Stephen O 20
Day, Sir Robin 48
democracy 4, 8
dictatorship 6, 9
Disqualification Act 1975 16
district council 36
Douglas-Home, Sir Alec *see* Home,
    Lord

Early Day Motion 20
Eden, Sir Anthony 35
election agents 53, 54
election campaigns 54
election, general 10, 52–9
electoral boundaries 43, 44–5
electoral register 52–3
electoral systems 56–8
electorate, growth of 43–4
Elizabeth II **12** *see also* monarch
European Communities Act 1972 12
expulsion from party 20, 29
extremist groups 32

Falklands war **25**, 50
Fawcett, Millicent 43
'first past the post' system 56
France 48, 57
Franco, Francisco 6

'Gang of Four' **20**, 21
Germany, East (German Democratic
    Republic) 5
Germany, West (Federal Republic of
    Germany) 57
Giscard d'Estaing, Valéry 48
Grant, Bernie **37**

Hailsham, Lord (Quintin Hogg) 35
Hamilton, Willie **13**
Hardie, Keir **31**

Harman, Harriet 22
Hatton, Derek **37**
Heath, Edward 11, **26**, 35
Heseltine, Michael **25**, **27**
Hogg, Quintin *see* Hailsham, Lord
Home, Lord (Sir Alec Douglas-Home)
    14, **16**, 34, 35
honours 27

India 10
Industrial Relations Act 1971 11
inner Cabinet 24
Iran **6**
Ireland, Northern 32, 45, **53**
Ireland, Republic of 42, 58
Israel 57

Jenkins, Roy **20**, 21
Johnson Smith, Sir Geoffrey 48
judges 4, 10, 28

Keen, T L 17
Khomeini, Ayatollah **6**
Kilroy-Silk, Robert 48
Kinnock, Neil 34, **35**
Kruschev, Nikita 11

Labour: government 11, **20**, 45, 58;
    Party 14, 18–19, **30**, 31, 32, 34–5, **37**,
    46–7, 55, **57**
Latin America 6
law 10, 11, 12, 15
Leigh-Smith, Barbara 43
Liberal Party 18–19, 22, 30, 31, 32, 34,
    47, 55, 58
Liverpool local government **37**
Livingstone, Ken **39**
Lloyd George, David 47
Local Authorities Act 1985 36
local government: Bains Report 39;
    councillors 36, 38; finance 40–41;
    Liverpool 37; London 36, **37**, **39**;
    organisation 36–9; services 40–41;
    staff 38
Local Government Act 1972 36
local politics *see* constituency; local
    government; parties political
London local government 36, **37**, **39**
Lords, House of 10, 14, **15**, 42 *see also*
    Parliament

MacDonald, Ramsay **31**

Macmillan, Harold 34, 35
Magna Carta 10
manifesto 55
Marcos, Ferdinand **7**
Maudling, Reginald 35
media (press and broadcasting) 8, 24, 26, 48–51
Members of Parliament: activities 20; ages 18; candidates 17, 25, 52–3; change of Party 23; education 18; eligibility to become 16; occupations 19; pay 20; resignation 23; women 21
metropolitan county councils 36
Militant Tendency **37**
Mill, John Stuart 43
Milne, Edward 20
monarch 10, 12–13, 26, 59 *see also* Elizabeth II
Mulhearn, Tony **37**

National Front 32, **40**
National Union of Mineworkers 31
nationalized industries 27, **31**
News International **11**
newspapers *see* media
1922 Committee 33
Nixon, Richard 48
Northstead, Manor of 23

opinion polls 55
Owen, David **20**, 21

pairing 29
Paisley, Ian **17**
parish council 36
Parliament: committees 28–9; history 14; law-making 12; sovereignty 11; summoning and dissolution 10; *see also* Acts of Parliament; Commons, House of; Lords, House of; Members of Parliament
Parris, Matthew 48
Parties, political: candidates for Parliament 17; committees 29; conferences 33; definition 5; expulsion from 20, 29; history 30–31; leader 34–5; local 32, 38; MPs who change 21, 23; organization 32–3; share of votes

56; slogans 55; system 8, 20, 30–35 *see also* names of parties
Peerage Act 1963 **14**
'party list' system 57
Peoples' Democracies 5, 8, 36, 49
Philippines **7**
Plaid Cymru 32
Poland 5
police 4, **50**
polling stations 52–3, **59**
presiding officer 53, 59
Prime Minister: appointment and resignation 59; appointments made by 12, 24, 27–8; power 25, 28; responsibilites 26–7
privatization **31**
proportional representation 58

Queen *see* Elizabeth II; monarch

radio *see* media
rate-capping 41
rates 41
Reagan, Ronald **27**
recount 59
Redmayne, Sir Martin 35
Reece, Gordon **49**
referendum 5, 8
Reform Acts 1832–1969 42, 43, 46
Representation of the People Acts 1884–1985 10, 42, 43, 44

reshuffling 24, 26, 28
resignation from Parliament 23
returning officer 52, 59
Revolutionary Communist Party 32
Rodgers, William (Bill) **20**, 21
Rome, ancient 6
Rotten Boroughs 42
Runcie, Robert (Archbishop of Canterbury) **28**
Russell, Lord John **42**
Russia **4**, 10–11, 49

Saatchi and Saatchi 26, 32, **49**
Scotland 32, 45
Scottish National Party 32
'second ballot' system 57
security services 27, 28, **50**
select committees 28

shadow cabinet 24
'single transferable vote' system 58
slogans 56
Snowden, Philip **31**
Social Democratic and Labour Party 32
Social Democratic Party **20**, 21, 22, 31, 32, 34, 47, 58
socialism 31
Southall, outbreaks of violence **40**
Spain 6
Speaker of the House of Commons 45
Stalin, Josef 10, 49
standing committees 28
Star Wars **27**
Suffragette movement 43, **44**
Switzerland 5

Taverne, R (Dick) 20
television *see* media
Thatcher, Margaret 10, 12, 21, **24**, 26, 34, 35, **49**
Tories 30, 31
trade unions 11, 12, 18, 31, 34

Ulster Unionist Party 32
United States of America **27**, 48

Voting: behaviour of electorate 46–7; counting 59; eligibility 15, 42–4; Paties' share of votes 56; procedure 52–3, 59

Wakeham, John **29**
Walden, Brian 48
Walesa, Lech **5**
Wales 32, 45
Watergate 48
Weinberger, Casper (US Defence Secretary) **27**
Westland **25**
Whigs 30
Whips 26, 29
Whitehead, Phillip 48
Williams, Shirley **20**, 21
Wilson, Harold 11, **12**, **26**, **27**, 35
women: in Parliament 21–2; suffrage 43, **44**; voting habits 47
Workers' Revolutionary Party 32

Picture credits

BBC Enterprises *74*
Camera Press *Cover picture, 7, 15, 16, 17, 25, 28, 32, 33, 37, 38, 40, 41, 49, 51, 57, 59*
COI *24*
Mary Evans Picture Library *44, 52, 56*
The Labour Party *30, 31, 83*
Magnum *46*
Mansell Collection *4, 10, 42, 44, 58*
Photo Source *27, 46, 55*
Popperfoto *5, 6, 9, 11, 12, 13, 14, 17, 21, 22, 23, 25, 26, 27, 28, 29, 31, 34, 39, 53*
Press Association *12, 50*
SDP *20, 21*
Rex Photos *11, 35, 45, 49, 54, 55*

Acknowledgements

Charts on pp18, 19 are from *New Society* 'Society Today' March, 1980. The chart on p43 is from *Parliament and its Work* by Keith Marden, Wheaton, Exeter, 1979.
The producers would like to thank Professor Ivor Crewe for his help in the course of compilation.